TIN TABERNACLES

CORRUGATED IRON MISSION HALLS, CHURCHES & CHAPELS OF BRITAIN

Disused corrugated
iron church in Alma
Road, Enfield

TIN TABERNACLES
CORRUGATED IRON MISSION HALLS, CHURCHES & CHAPELS OF BRITAIN

IAN SMITH

CAMROSE
organisation

Published by Camrose Organisation

© Ian Smith 2004

ISBN: 0-9547126-0-9

Typeset in Garamond and Gill Sans

Printed by BAS Printers, Salisbury, Wiltshire

www.tintabernacles.com

St Clement's Church Hall, Neyland, Pembrokeshire

CONTENTS

Peeling paint,
Apostolic Church,
Pembroke

ACKNOWLEDGMENTS

All of the photographs in this book are by the author unless stated otherwise. All of the archive photographs are from the collection of John Bray unless stated otherwise. I would like to sincerely thank the following individuals and organisations in no particular order without whose help this book would not have been possible: Joanna Power, Alan Terrill, Louise Crossman, Liz Induni, John Dixon, author of *Look Back in Wonder*, Linda Ware; the children of the late Brynmor Pierce Jones, author of *How Lovely Are Thy Dwellings*; Philip Griffiths, Keith Thomas, Peter Wardle, Muriel Steer, Brian Wood, Phil Draper for his photographs, encouragement and inspired emails, Richard Hawkins, Revd. Nigel Lemon, Rosalind Kaye, Doug Glading, Marion Hall, Andrew Smith, Sandy Wright, Robin Lee, Doug Jones, Hilary Jackson, David Nunn, Christopher Wilson, David Haggan, Sue Hadley, Doreen Aston, author of *A History of Brentwood Church*, Colin Hicks, Ian Viles, WCE Lindley, Brigit Carlstein and Annette Coetzee at the McGregor Museum in Kimberley, South Africa, Valerie Regel, editor of *100 Years Young*, John Bray who provided most of the archive postcards from his own extensive collection of church views, Miles Cowsill, Michael Stanway, Neil Marchant, David Taylor, Carolyn Adey, John Hendy, Margaret Brace, John Wittich, Janice Cox, Christopher Powell, Gwyn Powell, Simon Knott, Mike Andrews, Catherine Taylor and John Wittich for the use of their excellent photographs and information and my proof reader, Maddy Rowe. I would like to extend my sincere apologies to anyone I have inadvertently forgotten.

Organisations like Capel in Wales (Cymdeithas Treftadaeth y Capeli/The Chapels Heritage Society), The Chapels Society (who seek to promote public interest and knowledge of the architectural and historic importance of non-conformist places of worship) and the Ecclesiological Society also provided access to very valuable information as well as learned members and I would recommend anyone with an interest in ecclesiastic buildings whether as a lay person or not to join either organisation.

My particular thanks must go to Air Vice Marshall Sir John Severne KCVO OBE AFC DL, who passed on his own excellent and extensive collection of data about the subject and also showed both myself and my family great hospitality when visiting him at Alhampton. I must also thank Dr John R Salmon who not only allowed me to use some of his excellent photographs but also spent a great deal of his time sourcing and providing archive material. Jim Miller kindly let me use some of his beautiful images of tin churches in Iceland which he photographed while stationed there with the US government. He also read the text about Iceland and provided valuable tips about Icelandic spellings and typographic differences.

Every person I have approached or corresponded with during the research for this book has been both courteous and interested. I would like to thank each and every one of them personally but unfortunately space permits me only to thank them as a group.

Finally I would like to dedicate this book to the memory of my mother Esther and to my patient and understanding wife Joy, and my children George and Millie.

Ian Smith, Pembroke, 2004

367
311
197
205

Interior of
Alhampton Church
near Ditcheat

INTRODUCTION

This book began as the germ of an idea about ten years ago. Having stumbled across a few of these corrugated iron buildings some of which retained an obvious grandeur belied by their current outward appearance, I was struck by their charm and aesthetic beauty – not to everyone's taste but beauty, after all, *is* in the eye of the beholder. I thought at the time that the examples I had seen were certainly photogenic in a gritty industrial way that most church buildings were not and I imagined that a series of such pictures might make an interesting photographic exhibition.

Due to other commitments, this notion remained just an idea until recently when I began to research the subject in more detail. I soon realised what an enormous task I had set for myself. As well as documenting existing examples, I found it necessary to research some of the disused buildings and then more and more information came to light about other corrugated ecclesiastical buildings which had been demolished years before. The further into the subject I went, the larger it became. Fortunately it also became even more interesting and I began to realise that I would not only have to explain some of my personal fascination with these buildings but would also have to provide some social, economic and religious history about the buildings and the reasons which drove people to build them.

As the learning curve steepened I sought help from various sources but many of my initial contacts were made via the internet. A small research site was built (www.tintabernacles.com) to solicit information from interested individuals. Some contact with organisations like Capel in Wales (Cymdeithas Treftadaeth y Capeli/The Chapels Heritage Society), Cadw (Welsh Historic Monuments) and The Chapels Society (who seek to promote public interest and knowledge of the architectural and historic importance of non-conformist places of worship) provided some answers and yet more questions. Ultimately through the generosity of a number of interested individuals including lay people as well as those belonging to various religious denominations I was able to gather enough information to begin to tell the story of these 'tin tabernacles'. This book is far from exhaustive but I hope that amongst the jumble of facts and pictures brought together in it, there will be enough of interest to stimulate further research into the subject and also perhaps to aid the preservation of a few more of these marvellous little buildings.

All Saints',
Three Legged Cross,
Dorset

All Saints',
Beaconsfield Road,
Southall

This rather grand full size church has
done everything to try and emulate its
more permanent counterparts.
Unfortunately very few tin churches
of this size survive.

Chapter 1

Freshfield Congregational Church in Formby, Lancashire seen here c1908.

THE GREAT REVIVALS

Out of the seething white heat of the industrial revolution shone the equally intense light of religious revival. It is hard to envisage just how much influence religion had in the day to day lives of people just over one hundred and fifty years ago. David Barnes stated in his book *People of Seion* that a major purpose of his study of religious patterns was 'to attempt some explanation for the significance of a remarkable phenomenon which

Tin church at Baldslow,
(St Leonards on Sea), Sussex

Baptist Chapel, Banstead, Surrey

The Church of the Ascension, Bedmond, Nr Abbots Langley, Hertfordshire

This charming and secluded church built in 1880 and presented to the locals by William H Solly of Serge Hill to 'cater for the spiritual life of the people' can still be found just a few miles north of Watford on a recommended local walk.

The Mission Church at Beech, Nr Alton, Hants

The lady near the lamp post is obviously standing still for the photograph but her slightly blurred dog has not been so co-operative.

produced a vast outpouring of polemical literature virtually impenetrable to the late twentieth-century cast of mind'. A casual visit to almost any second hand book shop will turn up large numbers of books published to educate and inform the working man by a seemingly endless number of religious tract organisations as well as many more erudite books which are indeed almost incomprehensible in a modern context.

After the industrial progress made during Victoria's reign it is natural to think that the majority of the British working class would be better off in the closing years of the nineteenth century. A series of studies and reports at the time showed that this was not necessarily so. The cities were certainly cleaner and many of the upper working class homes now had gas and even electricity but there were still large sections of the population living in slum conditions below the poverty line and a number of religious organisations expressed concern. In 'The Bitter Cry of Outcast London' (1883) the London Congregational

St Mark's Tabernacle,
Biggin Hill, Nr Bromley, Kent

What are the two men in the top left hand side of the picture doing up the telegraph pole?

Union painted a grim picture. Twelve years earlier William Booth, founder of the Salvation Army, had described appalling conditions in his book 'In Darkest England and the Way Out'. Even the American author Jack London in 1903 published his account of living as one of the homeless in London's East End. The situation was similar across the country. The 1891 census showed that in Newcastle and Sunderland a third of the local population lived in overcrowded conditions. In Scotland as much as forty five per cent of the population shared overcrowded accommodation – the situation was hardly better twenty years later in the 1911 census. Juvenile deaths (children under five) in industrialised centres were still running as high as 46 per cent of the total number of deaths in 1897 and rural areas, while substantially better off, still recorded death under five as between 23 and 29 per cent of the total number of deaths.

In a society driven forward by the industrial revolution and with a workforce moving further away from the land and

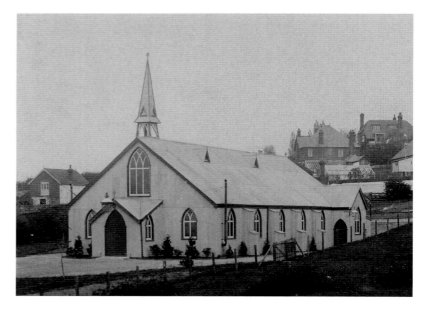

A very large Wesleyan Church at Bitterne Park, Southampton,

Bringsty Iron Church,
Bringsty Common,

Built in 1891 from a 12 metre long building kit supplied from a catalogue by JC Humphrey's Iron Yards and Works of Ludgate Station, London. The church has been re-erected at Avoncroft Museum of Historic Buildings in Herefordshire forty miles from its original site. The museum curator said at the time 'It represents an historic moment in architectural design – the introduction of corrugated iron as a new, durable building material. It is a perfect example of buildings which were once numerous all over the world'.

St Oswald's Church, Catterick Army Camp, Catterick

This view shows quite a large church built to cater for the spiritual needs of the men stationed at Catterick Camp.

whose needs were now being met by the money they could earn working long shifts for poor pay, it is easy to see how these same people would be ready for something to fulfil their spiritual needs. The industrial revolution not only revolutionised the capacity for manufactured production, it also revolutionised and changed forever the way people acquired the basic necessities of life. Instead of growing their own food or bartering with neighbours or at the local market, all the necessities of life had to be purchased with the money earned by the members of the workforce. Instead of working for the local squire and living in tied accommodation handed down the family from generation to generation, a working man had to pay rent, often to the company for which he worked. In these circumstances it is also easy to see how one might be tempted to spend a large amount of ones meagre earnings on drink to dull the pain of what might have been seen as an empty and unfulfilled life. This was certainly the churches view, both established and non-conformist, during the 19th century. To try and counteract this lapse in

Gospel Tent Mission seen every year in south Pembrokeshire

Cove Mission Church, Cove, Hants

Congregational Church, Walton on the Hill, Surrey

Interior of Cuffley Church, Hants

This large and rather grand interior view almost entirely disguises the fact that one is inside a corrugated metal building.

the spirituality of the population where towns supplied all the evils of nightlife: drink, prostitution and violence, the church supported by parliament and the landed gentry along with the new middle classes, sought ways to keep the working classes under control. During a time when the number of people attending church was beginning to decline, even in rural areas, an answer was looked for. It came in the form of a series of religious revivals spurred on by the non-conformists but the momentum did no harm to the established church apart from the establishment of a few more fervent splinter groups. Carried along with these revivals was the physical need to supply new places of worship. These evangelical movements, particularly the temperance movement, often started in a location with a tent. These tent missions drew crowds in to sign the pledge and were led by a preacher who was sometimes a woman. It is interesting to note that tent missions can occasionally still be found – one group makes regular visits to Pembrokeshire every summer continuing a mission started many years ago (see photos on page 5).

Interior and exterior of the Garrison Church at Deep Cut Camp, Surrey

As can be seen from the interior view, this was another very large tin tabernacle catering for the army personnel stationed at the garrison.

Deep Cut Camp, Garrison Church.

During the end of the nineteenth century whole communities could be moved from one part of the country where there was no work to another part where work was plentiful. The new arrivals often had slightly different religious beliefs or even, in some circumstances, different languages (English workers moving to Wales and vice versa). Even where the beliefs were compatible the increase in congregation numbers meant that a new building needed to be built. In Pembrokeshire when the new dockyard and ship building facilities came into being at Pembroke Dock, workers were recruited from the ship building ports of England. Many of these new arrivals from Portsmouth and Plymouth were Quakers or Plymouth Brethren and there was no suitable building where they could worship in their new home area. The men raised money themselves and through local appeals and finally built the Mission near Pembroke railway station which was opened by the Mayor of Pembroke in 1913 (photograph on page 150). This has changed hands over the years and is now the Pembroke Apostolic Church but it is still in regular use today nearly one hundred years later.

All of this building was driven forward by the Revivals. From the beginning of the nineteenth century right through to the outbreak of the first world war, a series of religious revivals took place. Reasons for these revivals varied from an individual but spectacular conversion

St Saviours Mission Church, Dottery, Nr Bridport, Dorset

The building of the church at Dottery was begun in November 1881 and finally completed in January 1882. Well hidden just short of the Bridport, Broadwindsor, Broadoak cross roads the church features an interesting pointed roof and small bell tower. A porch at the front protects from the wind and rain. The seating inside is plain benchwork either side and there is a small font. At the east end is a clergy stall with a pulpit behind. The west side houses the traditional harmonium. On the clergy desk is a magnificent prayer book donated by Edersheim (the original Vicar of Jewish origins). For use on the altar is a book of altar services with a beautiful carved wooden cover. Queen Victoria's name is still in situ so that the unwary priest can pray for 'they servant, Victoria, our Queen'. Behind altar is restored Reredos. Behind clergy stall is small vestry with just room for table, cupboard and priest. A small but loyal congregation meets here on the first and third Sundays of the month.

Left: Downely Church, Nr High Wycombe, Buckinghamshire

Above: Church at Eastcombe, Gloucestershire

experience through to mass experiences of 'heavenly singing' in the air heard at meetings attended by thousands of witnesses. Sermons preached by extremely effective speakers also spurred on the revivals. The great national revival of 1858-9 followed on immediately from the same phenomenon that had happened a year earlier in the USA. Churches and chapels were filled to overflowing across the country. More chapels and churches sprang up everywhere. In places where a suitable building was not readily available, various other buildings were pressed into service. Miners at the Mynydd Newydd mine, Swansea set up a chapel 774 feet underground and railway station waiting rooms and even billiard halls and public house ante-rooms were also used. Over 100,000 people were converted during this one revival alone. Twenty per cent of this total were Anglican while the remainder were non-conformist. Such numbers of people were flocking to the churches during this period that a notable drop in public disorder offences, drunkenness and violence was recorded by the courts at the time. Other types of business designed to cater for mass audiences felt the pressure as the population left the public houses, music halls and

Emanuel Church, Carshalton, Surrey

The poster near the door advertises a temperance campaign being held in the 'Great Tent'.

Everton Church, Everton, Nr Lymington, Hants

This delightful rural scene makes one wonder what the man with the tricycle was delivering?

The 'Gypsy Church', Bramdean Common, Hants

Hidden in the woods of Bramdean Common this picturesque little tin tabernacle is still standing. Built in 1883 as a mission church to the gypsies who camped in the woods at this time, the church is still used occasionally and the annual ground rent of five pence is still paid. See the contemporary photograph on page 55.

Church of the Good Shepherd, Carshalton, Surrey

The church at Golden Green, Kent

TIN TABERNACLES
11

theatres to attend revivalist meetings. Some taverns apparently had to close due to lack of business.

These revivals were the culmination of a process which had begun in the previous century with non-conformist religions making large inroads into the popular consciousness. The papers were filled with questions about the meaning of all sorts of religious and philosophical questions. It was a popular pastime to discuss these issues and this pastime was not indulged in just by the well off sections of society. As the educational standards were growing, so too were the abilities to not only question the status quo but also to make informed decisions about some of the questions raised. The existing Church of England, while still maintaining an enormously powerful position both politically and in the day to day religious life of the people, was having a very hard time keeping pace with the changes in society during the nineteenth century. Based as it was on an inherited system of parishes, some of which encompassed areas stretching from one side of the country to the other and with church buildings which had essentially not changed for centuries, the church was a slow moving dinosaur in comparison to the speedier non-conformists. For instance, early in the nineteenth century the population of Leeds had swollen to 64,000 while the traditional church buildings could only

Church at Harold Wood, Essex

Thatched Church at Hestercombe, Somerset

This unusual tin church with a thatched roof was not unique. The one built at Babingley in Norfolk is still there – see the photograph on page 88.

Colour tinted postcard view of St Barbara's Church at Hilsea, Nr Portsmouth, Hants

Little Holland Church, Little Holland, Essex

Right: Brick-fronted tin Baptist Church at Horsham, West Sussex

Many congregations put up tin churches as a temporary structure while they
raised funds for a more permanent building. Some may never have been able to
raise the money they needed or perhaps they just wanted to present a grander
image so the fronts of some of these tin churches like this example built c1892
featured an ornate masonry facade. Examples survive – one was demolished only
last year in Neyland, Pembrokeshire and there is a large hall in Machynlleth with
a similar facade. The Sunday evening service on this particular day promises,
rather eerily, a 'Voice from beyond the grave'.

The iron church at Hundleton, South Pembrokeshire

Hundleton is a very small village so one has to wonder why such a large and
handsome church was built in such a rural location.

The Church and Sunday School Hall at Knaphill, Woking, Surrey

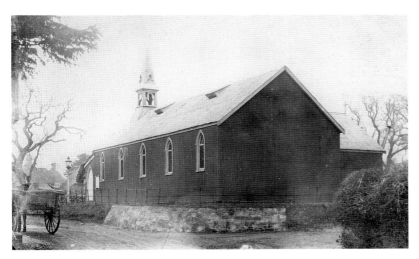

The church of St Joseph at Lower Froyle, Nr Alton, Hants (demolished in 1967) can be seen in these two views from about 1905.

cater for a congregation totalling 3,400. On a local level, St Mary's parish in Southampton could only cater for 650 people while the population had grown to 14,885 by 1841. This parish system had been upheld by a system of payments ranging from rent for pews through to tithes and contributions from the local gentry. The Church realised that it was rapidly losing ground and set upon a huge building programme which was intended to bring moral values to the vast industrial urban populations which were springing up. They also took this campaign into the countryside. The Church brought about a sea-change within society at this time.

As well as new buildings, many older buildings were restored and modernised. Services were also modernised, becoming more populist with more pomp and ceremony, the singing of hymns, more elaborate ritual, new pipe organs and greater audience participation. Peripheral activities by most churches also had a massive effect on their communities as parish and church magazines were published, picnics organised, soup kitchens set up, missions to cater for the poor and needy founded and Sunday and Day schools organised. Social work including the setting up of orphanages, temperance societies, clubs and friendly societies brought the church into much closer

Markby New Church, Markby, Lincolnshire

This church was quite large but unusually supported a slated roof.

The Monastery and Church at Martin, Hants

contact with the people. The underlying aim of all of this good work was to combat criminal behaviour, prostitution, alcoholism and violence amongst the working population which were all perceived to be on the increase. The following statistics illustrate not only the growing involvement with these problems by the Church of England, they also show the distinct upward trend in new building. Numbers of clergy between 1800 and 1841 also rose by 15,000 in the UK.

Melbourne Church, Melbourne, East Yorkshire

The magnificent white horse in front of the church could almost be a unicorn.

Left: large corrugated iron churches like this one at Clipston Camp, Nottinghamshire were built at many barracks across the UK. Churches like these were sometimes taken abroad and erected overseas by the army when engaged on long tours out of the country. Several survive.

Lee

The Wrench Series No. 5500

South Lee Tabernacle

South Lee Tabernacle, Lee, London

The Baptist School Room can be seen on the left behind the tabernacle.

Risely Church, Nr Swallowfield, Buckinghamshire

Anglican Church Building 1801-1870

	New churches	Rebuilt churches	Total consecrated churches
1801-10	28	15	43
1811-20	70	26	96
1821-30	235	73	308
1831-40	514	86	600
1841-50	759	170	929
1851-60	654	166	820
1861-70	791	319	1,110

(JH Bettey, Church and Parish: A Guide for Local Historians, Batsford 1987)

These figures only take us up to the 1870s but this exponential rise in the number of ecclesiastic buildings continued right through to the outbreak of the first world

St Agnes Church & Hall,
South Stoneham, Southampton

St George's Mission Church, West End, Esher, Surrey

The church can just be identified behind the well established rampant ivy.

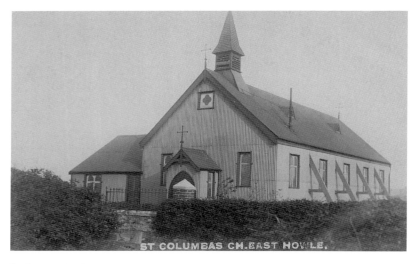

St Columba's Church, East Howle, Co Durham

Because of the way they are built, tin churches often have a tendency to lean or become skewed. This may explain the props along the near side. These flying buttresses can be seen in a number of old photographs as well as in several existing tin tabernacles. This church is still standing and has been used for agricultural storage for many years (photo page 57).

Above: this substantial mission room at Bury St Edmunds for railway workers and their families is dwarfed by some of the industrial buildings behind. This church has survived although the marvellous bell tower has not.

Left: interior view of St Alphege Church, Edmonton, London

Two exterior views and one interior view illustrating the size and grandness of the tin Church of Saints Peter & Paul nestling in the woods at Appuldurcombe, Isle of Wight

war. As well as all this building by the established church, the number of non-conformists chapels continued to rise with new buildings appearing across the country in both urban and rural locations. The differences between the Wesleyans, Primitive Methodists, Baptists, Moravians, Bible Christians, Calvinists, Unitarians, Independents, Particular Baptists, Methodists, Apostolics, Jehovah's Witnesses, Mormons, United Free Methodists, Pentecostals, Calvinistic Methodists, Plymouth Brethren, Quakers, Wesleyan Methodists, Dissenters, Presbyterians, and others who have disappeared in the mists of time would probably be lost on all but the most focused academic minds even in the nineteenth century but these

St George's Church at Headstone (Harrow), Middlesex

St Faith's Church at Lee-on-the-Solent, Hants

St Cuthbert's Church, Brislington, Bristol.

Exterior and interior views. The church features an unusually elegant bell housing which is a simple extension of the roof line. Note how the light and spacious interior belies the size of the exterior.

Exterior and interior views of the church of St James at Prickwillow, Cambridgeshire

very differences were undoubtedly part of the reason that new buildings continued to be erected.

The minute schisms between some of these non-conformists led to whole communities turning against each other and rival chapels sometimes being built across the road from the original chapel. The number of travelling preachers and mission organisers probably reached its peak towards the end of the nineteenth century and the good word was spread through tent missions, temperance societies, Sunday schools, Mothers' Union and various other organisations which have all become associated inextricably with the Revivals.

The Roman Catholic Church, not to be out done, also embarked on a campaign to ensure that it kept its congregations and even perhaps increase its numbers. A number of Catholic tin tabernacles still exist today.

St James' Church, Long Bennington, Lincolnshire

Another church being swallowed up by the creeping ivy. The small boy in front of the church was a well used ploy by early postcard photographers to lend charm and a sense of scale to pictures.

St John's Church, Ramsden Heath, Essex

St John's Church, Fishponds, Bristol

This church has tin-clad buttresses and quite modern looking sheeting on the roof.

St Patrick's Church,
Wallington, Surrey

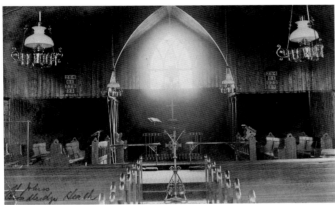

Against this background it is not difficult to see why the waves of religious revivals had so many converts. The hope and promise of a better life was very persuasive and while most people would probably have preferred more physical and immediate improvements in their lives, the idea of spiritual improvement must have provided some comfort. The missions responsible for building many of these tin halls also sprang from this unrest. The purpose of each mission may have differed – from temperance missions to get men to 'sign the pledge' and fight the evils of drink, through to literacy missions which set up 'reading rooms' to teach an illiterate population the skills for self improvement, but whatever the mission, there was a need for reasonably priced accommodation which could be built quickly and easily dismantled and used elsewhere if the need arose.

The Temperance Movements

These were one of the offshoots of the Revivals. Often started in tents by preachers from a diverse range of denominations, they were also often linked to the Sunday School movements which had been founded to educate the less well off. Alcohol was a persistent evil in the Victorian religious conscience. Temperance clubs were

Two interior and two exterior views of St John's Church at Broadbridge Heath, Sussex

The lower interior view shows flowers displayed across the church so was probably taken during Harvest Festival. The trellis work seen in the later exterior view makes it evident that the ivy was being encouraged to grow up the walls.

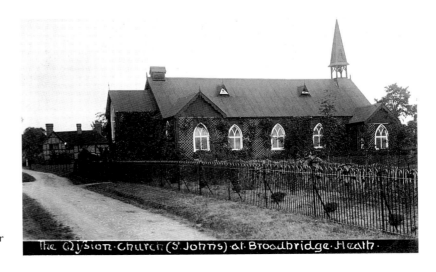

This delightful unidentified tin tabernacle appears to be standing in a rural setting near some farm buildings. Does anybody recognise this church or its location?

Views of St Mark's Church at Woodcote, Purley in Surrey

The sign outside the building (far right) is soliciting contributions towards the building of a new permanent church. The trellis work is in place ready for the ivy to begin growing.

St William's Church at Ince, Lancashire

This is another large church which features buttresses. These must have helped to keep the church from skewing or leaning – very important for a structure as large as this.

Totteridge Church, Nr High Wycombe, Buckinghamshire

Below and lower right: two rather different views of St Paulinus Church, Marlpit Hill, Edenbridge, Kent. Taken at different times, one shows a building which seems well established with hedges and foliage set in an almost urban environment while the earlier one shows the church in what appears to be a rural setting with trees showing little sign of growth yet.

formed across the country, and in fact the movement spread across the world at this time. Rooms were hired to sell soft drinks and offer entertainment to try and entice working men (and women) away from public houses. The author recalls drinking sarsaparilla – the temperance movement's answer to alcohol – in one of the last of these in Cardiff city centre which closed during the 1980s. The temperance cause was more formally taken up following the establishment of the 'Band of Hope Union' which had branches across the UK. This name was originally applied in 1847 by a Mrs Anne Carlile to groups of Sunday School children from Leeds who were organised as part of the temperance cause, the movement spread with much support from Nonconformists, from the cities and towns to the villages. The children were encouraged to offer a good example to their parents by the singing of temperance hymns

St Paulinus' Church & Parsonage, Marlpit Hill.   3.

Below: the delighfully rural church at Shirrell Heath has an old fashioned hay rick standing just next to it. It may have been a Methodist Church.

Shirrell Heath   3

Marlpit Hill Church, Edenbridge.

and reciting of temperance prayers. The Bands of Hope organised Temperance fêtes, Temperance days, performances and so on and the children were often excused from school to attend these events when they were held during weekday afternoons. Children were persuaded to 'sign the pledge' and although many went on to live a life with little or no drinking, the crusading efforts came to a virtual end following the outbreak of the first world war.

Interior of the Catholic Church of St Joseph's at Ushaw Moor, Co Durham

Three views of the little Mission Church at Wadhurst Station, Sussex

The railway line passing under the bridge can be seen quite clearly. Mission churches of this type were not uncommon and could be found near industrial sites across the country. They were built to bring the good word to the working classes.

Chapter 2

This unusual example of a corrugated iron Parish Church at Binchester seems to have been well established – the graveyard already held a number of occupants by the time the photograph was taken.

REVOLUTIONARY BUILDINGS

If you had walked through Britain at the end of the nineteenth century or beginning of the twentieth you might have noticed some very peculiar buildings in the midst of the 'dark satanic mills' and in the inaccessible parts of the agricultural heartland. Perhaps none were more strange than the 'Tin Tabernacles' – little churches and chapels which used to be so common across the UK. From a distance they appeared like many another religious building but on closer inspection they were found to be manufactured in one of the most modern materials of the

The Tin Church at Alsager

This view of St Aldhelm Roman Catholic Church at Turton features a priest in the doorway and an unusual cylindrical tower.

time: corrugated iron. In their heyday they were the life blood of the small communities they served. These industrially made Tin Churches rang out to the sounds of the great religious revivals over a period of several decades but the first world war spelled the beginning of the end for many of them.

The word tabernacle is derived from the Latin tabernaculum which means a booth, hut or temporary dwelling. In the scriptures it refers to the Jewish portable sanctuary erected by Moses and described in the book of Exodus. The Feast of Tabernacles still commemorates the dwellings of the Israelites as well as the ancient custom of living in temporary accommodation, especially during harvest times.

These buildings were purpose built to house the growing congregations who had been persuaded to return to the fold of Christianity during the Revivals. They were also built to be temporary and portable. In fact they were made to be dismantled and rebuilt so a number of them can be found in exotic locations overseas and even the ones still standing may have seen use in another location before reaching their final destination. Most of the 'Tin Tabernacles' were intended to provide short term accommodation while the pastor and his flock gathered

Above: this fine church is St Andrews, Felixstowe seen in about 1909. The interior view shows the quality of interior fittings and carpentry as well the intricate metal castings which make up parts of the roof trusses.

Tin Church at Hartlepool

funds for the building of a more permanent place of worship. These prefabricated buildings were used by many denominations even outside the sphere of Christianity; some were used as temporary synagogues. However they were predominantly mission halls used to take the good word out to either the urban heathens of the the new industrial society or to reach out into the agricultural community and provide religious enlightenment to the masses of farm workers too far away to attend their local 'high church'.

Usually sitting on a rudimentary brick or rubble and mortar foundation, these tin churches were based on a simple bolt-together wooden frame. The inside walls were lined with tongue and groove match board pine while the outer walls and roof were clad with corrugated iron sheeting. Flooring ranged from simple beaten earth or flagstones to suspended wooden floorboards. Windows were sometimes simple rectangular shapes but many had

Woodside Baptist, Woodside, Croydon

Opened on 4 September 1898, the Baptist Hall (then sometimes referred to as the Iron Building) was erected as a temporary structure while funds were raised for a 'proper' church. This was a Baptist church and the first baptismal service was conducted during December 1899. Sunday School was an important part of the life of this church as well as Mother's Meetings and Evangelist missions. The iron building held about 200 people but there were 332 children on the Sunday School register. Foundation stones for a new building were laid on 21 September 1905 and the new building was completed in 1906 although the original corrugated iron building was retained for a number of years as a church hall.
Photos courtesy of John Dixon/Don Stewart

BAPTIST CHURCH, WOODSIDE.   W.B FOREY.

exquisitely proportioned gothic arches with tracery windows in rows down the sides of the building echoing the more established church architecture. The more ornate example had a small steeple or bell tower to call the people to service and occasionally the roof had skylights or dormer windows or perhaps a clerestory to provide ventilation. Insulation was often in the form of felt placed between the outer and the inner walls.

Heating and lighting in the earliest tin churches was non-existent but lighting by paraffin lamp was followed by gas lighting in some of the more urban examples. Since many of these Tin Tabernacles had a non-conformist congregation who had deliberately turned away from the comfortable excesses of other churches, heating was probably seen as a comfort which they could do without and some surviving buildings in use today still have no heating. Those that were heated (and many were used as

TEDDINGTON BAPTIST CHAPEL
CHURCH ROAD.

OPENING SERVICES

Divine Service will be held (D.V.) on Sunday March 30th

ON THE FOLLOWING TUESDAY, APRIL 1st, 1884,

A SERMON
Will be Preached by the Rev

V. J. CHARLESWORTH,
OF THE REV. C. H. SPURGEON'S ORPHANAGE.

SERVICE TO COMMENCE AT 3 O'CLOCK.
AFTER WHICH,

TEA AND PUBLIC MEETING
WILL BE HELD

Tea at 5.30.   Tickets 1s. each.   Public Meeting at 7.
When ADDRESSES are expected from the Rev. W. BASTER (Surbiton). Rev. V. J.
CHARLESWORTH. Rev. J. DUNN (London). Revs. J. M. FOX & J. S. HAWORTH.
(Teddington). Rev. GEORGE WRIGHT (Kingston), and other Friends.

Chair to be taken by J. COWDY, Esq., of Molesey

Collections after each Service in aid of the Building Fund.

Baptist Church, Teddington
Photos courtesy of Colin Hicks

The Tin Tabernacle was used as the Teddington Baptist Church's only building from 1884–1907. A permanent church was begun in 1895 and the tin church was moved from its original site to an adjacent site to allow the construction of the new building. When the new church opened in 1896, the tin church was used for Sunday School until 1907. A new Sunday School was opened in 1907 and the tin tabernacle was probably dismantled and perhaps sold on at that time. The photo shows the building between 1896 and 1907.

MR. EVAN ROBERTS' MEETINGS.

REVIVAL.

WONDERFUL RESULTS OF THE MOVEMENT.

CONVERSIONS NUMBER OVER SEVENTY THOUSAND.

Place	No.	Place	No.	Place	No.
Aberaman	238	Fleur-de-lis, Pengam, and Gilfach	214	Penarth	600
Aberavon	325	Freystrop	35	Penclawdd	193
Aberbeeg	155	Ffrwdcymylle (N. W.)	60	Penderyn (Aberdare)	10
Abercrave	57	Gaebyn	147	Penrhiwceiber	433
Abercwmboy	140	Gwilliger	17	Pentre	1,382
Abercynon	630	Gilfachgoch	451	Penycae (N. Wales)	150
Aberdare	715	Gilwern and district	60	Penygraig	408
Abergwynfi and Blaengwynfi	420	Glyncorrwg	135	Penywaun (Aberdare)	50
Aberkenfig	256	Glyn-Neath	450	Peterstone	15
Abernant	97	Goodwick	20	Pontardawe	212
Abersychan, Pontnewynydd, Talywain, Garndiffaith, and Varteg	453	Gorseinon	304	Pontardulais	435
		Gowerton and Waunarlwydd	141	Pontlottyn	242
Abertillery, Sixbells, and Cwmtillery	2,342	Gwern-cae-Gurven	20	Pontnewydd	62
Abertridwr	98	Itstad	262	Pontrhydfendigaid	30
Aberystwyth and district	220	Haverfordwest	90	Pontrhydyfen	12
Barry	424	Heolycyw	22	Pontrhydygroes	20
Bargoed	162	Hirwain and district	327	Pontyberem	102
Beaufort	100	Hopkinstown	84	Pontyclun and district	120
Bedling	182	Kenfig Hill	498	Pontycymmer	810
Bedwas	39	Kidwelly	191	Pontygwaith	270
Blackwood	340	Lampeter and district	110	Pontypool	407
Blaenavon	810	Landore	746	Pontypridd	1,645
Blaenconin (Pem.)	6	Laugharne & Plasket	80	Pontyrhyl	98
Blaengarw	545	Llanbradach	194	Porth	658
Blaenpennal	15	Llanddewi-Brefi	40	Porthcawl	49
Blaina	878	Llandilo (Pem.)	12	Pyle	61
Bontnewydd (near Aberayron)	15	Llandovery	87	Resolven	661
Bridgend	279	Llandrindod Wells and Howey Village	10	Rhondda	100
Briton Ferry	406	Llandyssul and district	114	Rhuddlan	13
Bryncethin	86	Llanelly, Loughor, and Felinfoel	1,317	Rhydfelen	95
Brynmawr	274	Llanelly Hill (Brecon)	90	Rhyl (N. Wales)	45
Brynmenin	22	Llangattock	53	Rhymney	770
Builth Wells	163	Llangeitho	45	Risca	630
Burry Port	264	Llangenech	68	Robertstown	82
Bwlchgwyn	30	Llangollen (N. W.)	54	Regerstone	400
Caerphilly	685	Llangyfelach	24	St. Asaph (N. Wales)	8
Capcoch	45	Llanharan	245	St. Bride's	21
Cardiff	1,068	Llanhilleth	182	St. Clears	88
Cardigan and district	300	Llaniddea	27	St. David's	38
Carmarthen	75	Llannon	17	St. Fagan's	50
Cefncribwr	75	Llansamlet	274	St. Mellon's	32
Cilfrew and Coytant	101	Llantwit Major	138	Sardis (Pem.)	30
Cilfynydd	721	Llwydcoed	87	Senghenydd	487
Clydach (Brecon)	56	Llwynhendy	109	Seven Sisters and Onllwyn	121
Clydach-on-Tawe	270	Llwynypod	25	Skewen	481
Clydach Vale	689	Llwynypia	112	Sutton (Pem.)	27
Coedpoeth	70	Machen	209	Swansea	500
Coity	23	Maesteg	2,115	Talbach and Margam	270
Cowbridge	26	Maenclochog	60	Talgarth and district	84
Coychurch, Troos, and Llankan	70	Maesycwmmer	188	Talywain	74
Crickhowell	91	Maindee (Newport)	8	Tongwynlais	135
Crosshands and Tumble	278	Mardy	680	Tonna and Aberdulais	102
Crosskeys	600	Merthyr	760	Tonypandy	340
Crumlin	18	Merthyr Vale	874	Tonyrefail	301
Cwmaman	565	Middle Hill (Haverfordwest)	38	Trealaw	15
Cwmamman (Carm.)	471	Milford Haven	100	Trebanos	50
Cwmbach	374	Miskin	12	Treecnon	516
Cwmbran	323	Morriston	1,068	Tredegar	1,500
Cwmdare	93	Mountain Ash	778	Treforest	58
Cwmgwrach	111	Mynyddbach	14	Tregaron	60
Cwmllynfell	120	Nantymoel	58	Treharris	1,003
Cwmpark ... dir	135	Nantygio	307	Treherbert, Blaenrhondda, and Blaenycwm	1,164
Cymmer	79	Neath	1,205	Treorky	1,488
Dowlais and Penydarren	1,265	Neath Abbey	71	Troedyrhiw	468
Dreflach and Velindre	89	Nelson	293	Tylorstown	650
Ebbw Vale	1,500	Newbridge	410	Walton West (Pem.)	50
Ferndale and Blaenllechau	700	New Milford	300	Watford (near Caerphilly)	47
Ferryside	17	New Quay	55	West Hook (Pem.)	32
Fforestfach & Cockett	286	Newport	900	Whitchurch	176
Fishguard	120	Newtown (N. Wales)	102	Ynyshir	458
		New Tredegar	301	Ynysybwl	792
		Ogmore Vale	28	Ystalyfera	392
		Pembrey and Pwll	160	Ystradgynlais	618
		Pembroke	12		
		Pembroke Dock	20	**Total**	**65,319**

Cutting from the Western Mail of 28th January 1905 which shows the effect that the Revival Meetings were continuing to have in Wales. It also illustrates the seriousness attached to the business of persuading people to turn over a new leaf. With conversion rates like this it becomes easy to see where the enthusiasm (and funding) for the building of new churches came from.

Sunday schools) often had a small coal or wood burning stove in one corner or a gas fire if town gas was available.

To keep these buildings in a historical context it is important to remember that corrugated iron was a very modern building material in the nineteenth century. Corrugated iron was being mass produced in England as early as c1830 by Richard Walker in his Bermondsey based 'patent corrugated iron factory'. The corrugations add an enormous amount of stiffness and structural integrity to the material. The sheets were sometimes galvanised, a process invented in France in 1837 which adds a coating of zinc to the sheets, preventing corrosion and giving the sheets a substantially longer life. The British Galvanisation of Metals Company was formed in 1839 and although 'galvanisation' is a misnomer, the name has entered the English language and become permanent. The buildings themselves were often bought in a form that we would recognise today as a do-it-yourself flat pack. Builders merchants like Charles D Young and Company of Edinburgh supplied complete kits of parts to meet the constructional needs of new congregations everywhere. Whilst at least a score of other companies undoubtedly had similar products, it was Boulton & Paul with a head office in Norwich and a network of joinery companies across England and Wales who probably supplied the bulk of these prefabricated churches. As they stated in their 1902 catalogue 'Although not so artistic or good looking as wood, iron churches are at the same time quite as serviceable, while the cost is less'. Because Boulton & Paul also built railway wagons for the massively expanding railway network, it is likely that their chapels would have been delivered by rail although many manufacturers priced their buildings as 'delivered to nearest rail head or wharf'. It is interesting to note, as an aside, that a number of railway wagons were also built clad with corrugated iron and the railwaymen also referred to these as Tin Tabs, an obvious abbreviation.

These tin buildings form an important but frequently

overlooked area of our ecclesiastical architectural heritage. 'The first was built in London in 1855 and their period is the end of the nineteenth century up to the Great War,' claims John Bracey who has studied them. 'I believe that tin tabernacles should be recognised as listed buildings, particularly as examples of prefabrication'. Despite this being the main period of building, tin churches were still being built in the 1920s and even 1930s and a number of ex-military corrugated iron huts were pressed into service as church halls well into the twentieth century.

Prices for these church kits began at under £100.00 and the building would often be undertaken by the congregation over a period of several weekends. This must have been reminiscent of an American barn-raising bee with plenty of food, non-alcoholic drink and uplifting song. The foundations would be arranged first on a piece of land often begged or borrowed from a local landowner, farmer or industrialist at a peppercorn ground rent (one deed cites a 999 year lease for 1 shilling) which explains why so many of the remaining tin churches have such a small area of land around them. The land would be levelled and a base of brick or rubble and mortar prepared followed by the erection of the timber frame which just bolted together. Once this structure was in place it is likely that the roof would follow so that the remaining joinery and other work could be finished under cover: a good idea in a British climate. Internal fittings and furnishings would have been simple benches initially with perhaps a small raised platform at one end for the preacher or pastor. The match board walls would have received a few coats of whitewash and perhaps a few prints illustrating scenes from the bible. Tin Tabernacles which began to become permanent structures perhaps because funds for a 'proper' church could not be found or the active membership numbers fell, undoubtedly had the quality of their internal fittings raised over the years to the point where some resembled a small parish church complete with pews and a pulpit. Some of these chapels featured quite ornate carvings on their timber work, often applied by a local amateur craftsman

William Cooper was one of a number of horticultural suppliers who offered corrugated iron buildings in its advertisements and catalogues. £100 would buy you a 40 ft x 20 ft church building delivered and erected on your pre-prepared foundations.

J.C. Humphreys was another manufacturer offering iron churches, chapels, portable iron houses and a variety of other buildings for sale during the late nineteenth and early twentieth centuries.

who suddenly found an appreciative audience for his work.

Prefabricated church buildings were advertised regularly in the 'Freeman' periodical during the end of the nineteenth and beginning of the twentieth centuries and could also be found advertised in many other religious society publications during the time. There was such an enormous amount of religious literature published during the nineteenth century that the advertising and marketing of these buildings must have been quite an easy job.

This was also the time of pioneering colonisation across the world and the British Empire was expanding at such a rate that many manufacturers specialised in the export of buildings overseas. It was common practice to actually build the complete structure in the manufacturer's yard after which it would be dismantled, packed and sold. Opportunities like the Californian Gold Rush and the great Australian Gold Strike which took place at about the same

Christ Church, Black Gang, Isle of Wight

One of several tin churches found on the Isle of Wight during the early years of the twentieth century. The other one is the unusually double-dedicated Church of Saints Peter & Paul at Appuldurcombe.

Christ Church, Black Gang, I.W.

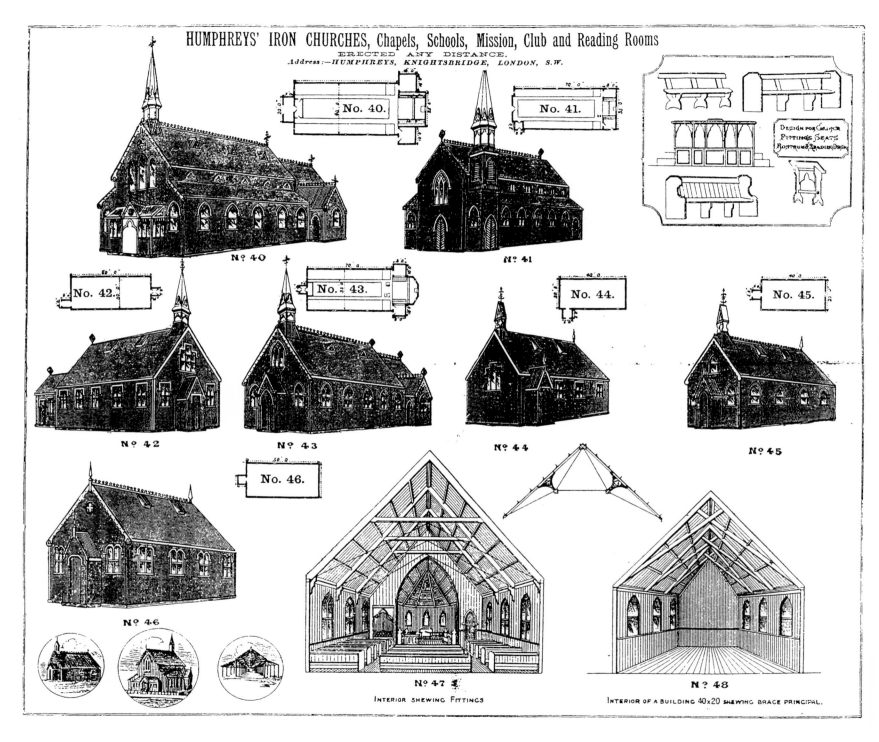

A sample page from one of the Humphreys catalogues shows just a few of the bewildering variety of offerings. As well as churches and chapels, most of these manufacturers also offered hospitals, asylums, servants' quarters, bungalows, gardeners' lodgings, cricket pavilions and billiards rooms along with houses, hotels, restaurants and cook houses. Their portability meant that they were taken all over the world during colonisation, gold rushes and wars.

Iron Churches, &c. xi

CHURCH AND SCHOOL EXTENSION. MISSION WORK

DIXON'S
IRON CHURCHES, CHAPELS, MISSION ROOMS,
SCHOOLS, LECTURE & TEMPERANCE HALLS, &c. &c.

Are tasteful in design, economical, durable, made of the best materials, and erected in the most careful manner. Can be taken down, removed, and re-erected at small cost.

IRON CHURCHES &c. Usually on hand, or in progress at the Works.

IRON BUILDINGS For all purposes and all climates.

Careful comparison of Specifications, Structural and Architectural Details, Materials, and Workmanship is invited before placing orders.

Catalogues, Designs, Estimates, and all information on application to

ISAAC DIXON & CO., Windsor Iron Works, Spekeland Road, LIVERPOOL.

St James' Church, New Farnley, near Leeds

With the foundation of the Farnley Iron Works in 1844, by the four Armitage brothers, came the building of New Farnley village. For the convenience of the villagers an unconsecrated Church named after St. James was built in 1863 above the Iron Works. Constructed from corrugated iron it was financed by clergy stipends paid for by the Farnley Iron Company. The church was built in Whitehall Road on land given by the Earl of Cardigan. It was known locally as 'the tin church'. It had a short chancel or sanctuary with a vestry and organ chamber and there was an iron gable for one bell. Paper transparencies simulated stained glass. Even the lychgate appears to have a corrugated roof. This card was postally used in 1910 but the photograph appears to be much earlier. The building was replaced in 1959.

Isaac Dixon & Co promoted their wares in advertisements like this one. St Philip's Church, Hassall Green, near Haslington, Cheshire was built by them and can still be seen today with its original manufacturer's plates (see page 72).

time during the nineteenth century were fully exploited by the manufacturers of prefabricated buildings. These companies not only made churches but also hospitals, housing, hotels, servants' quarters, bunkhouses, in fact almost any type of building one wished for could be bought 'off the peg' and ready to be erected. King Eyambo had an 'Iron Palace' built for himself by Lacock of Liverpool in 1845 and before it was exported to Africa it was exhibited to the public who paid an entry fee to view it (all takings went to charity). Prince Albert had a ballroom constructed at Balmoral Castle by a company called Bellhouse who also built a Customs House and General Store for export to South America which was viewed by over 25,000 people in a period of ten days before being shipped abroad.

A number of the large British engineering companies showed iron buildings at The Great Exhibition at Crystal Palace in 1851. The first iron church is reported to have been erected in the grounds of the vicarage at Kensington in London. The industry kept on expanding during this period and probably reached a peak of production during the 1880s. A later resurgence of the use of corrugated iron took place when Lt Col PN Nissen designed a hut for military use and many of these can still be seen in the UK but the majority of these corrugated iron buildings have long since disappeared and they are already a forgotten memory. However, for some reason, the church buildings have lingered on far longer than most of the other types. There are probably more churches, chapels and mission halls, along with peripheral buildings like school rooms, reading rooms and temperance halls still in use in the UK than most people would imagine.

Waterhouses Mission Room, Waterhouses, Co Durham

The church hall of St Paul's was opened in 1891. The building has a main hall
with a kitchen to the rear and toilets in the side porch. The hall is still being used
regularly for events and meetings.

The church seen here at Earby in about 1904 (denomination unknown) in West
Yorkshire is quite large and features corrugated iron buttresses which help shore
up the building and prevent it from twisting or skewing. It was not unusual for
smaller tin churches to bend or blow right down in adverse weather conditions.

Chapter 3

ENGLAND

Who built them?

Construction of these churches ranges from the simplest rectangular hut to incredibly ornate attempts at replicating grand 'high church' architecture using the simple wooden frame clad in corrugated iron. Most mission chapels were bought in what we would recognise today as self assembly flat packs. The timber frame was bolted together, usually by volunteer labour from the congregation. The roof was put on first so that work could progress under cover if necessary. The outsides were clad in corrugated iron while the inner walls were usually tongue and groove raw pine which was simply whitewashed. Internal seating was

St Paul's Mission Church, Warren Row, between Reading and Maidenhead

St Paul's Mission Church was bought from one of the leading iron church manufacturers, JG Humphreys Ltd, Knightsbridge, London for £104-14s-0d in 1894 and erected and consecrated on 6 October the same year by the Bishop of Reading. It has been used continuously since then and it is still looked after with pride by its local community.
Photos David Nunn

St David's Church, Tudhoe, Co Durham

The Parish of Tudhoe was created in 1866 at which time the Holy Innocents Church was built to cater for the local population. However by 1880 it became necessary to build another church to cater for the parishioners at Tudhoe and its main source of employment, the colliery. The corrugated iron St David's Church was built in 1880 on land leased from MC Salvin at £1 per year. Designed originally to seat around 280, it cost £610 to purchase but it was enlarged in 1882 and again in 1885 after which it could hold a congregation of 313. It is now re-clad in modern box section corrugated steel but the charm of the original building has not been lost as it has been particularly well maintained.

St James, Vines Cross, Sussex

The small corrugated church building in Vines Cross features an unusual separate roofed bell tower.
Photo Mike Fradd

Mission Hall in Hyde Road, Swindon
Yet another mission church seeing out its final days in a state of dereliction.
Photo Doug Jones

equally rustic – often simple benches while the front of the church would have a simple altar, sometimes a pulpit or low stage depending on the denomination. Some Baptist churches had a total immersion font installed internally. Windows also ranged from the simple square cornered to gothic arched varieties and the glass was ribbed, rippled, frosted and occasionally stained (although most of the extant tin churches with stained glass windows had the stained glass installed at a later date – frugal Victorians would have been saving their money for the 'permanent' church building).

Building in general did not slow down until the end of the nineteenth century. The advent of new materials combined with commercialism even in the sphere of church life brought about a completely new type of church building. From about the 1870s, prefabricated buildings became available which combined ease of erection through the use of simple timber framing with the relatively new and lightweight (compared to masonry) corrugated iron sheeting. Quite apart from the corrugated metal buildings which were actually used as places of worship (churches or chapels) no end of similar buildings had direct connections with the church. These buildings were used as Sunday Schools, Day Schools, Church Halls, Temperance Missions, and a variety of other less religious uses.

Diocesan records for the Bristol area detail the consecration of a number of temporary iron churches erected as an interim measure while money was being raised for permanent churches. Some of these buildings were manufactured by local ironfounder company Acramans and similar manufacturers were jumping on the prefabricated church bandwagon across the country.

By the middle of the nineteenth century more than half the world's iron was being produced in Britain. At the same time about 60 per cent of the global shipping tonnage was also British. The economy of the nation was continually

All Saints Church, Thrupp,
Gloucestershire

Very large tin church built in 1889 by
Messrs Humphreys, Iron Church
Builders of Knightsbridge with
stained glass windows and buttresses
clad in corrugated iron. Must have
been a very imposing building in its
day but is now in a very poor state
of repair and does not look as if it
has been used for some time. The
entrance doors were completely
overgrown and some of the windows
had been broken. The edge of the
roof stands at street level as the
church is built on a steep slope.
Security fencing and barbed wire have
been added to stop people climbing
up the roof (anyone doing this was
obviously attempting an early
appointment with his maker).

Tin hall at Tiverton photographed in passing. Nothing on the outside of this corrugated iron hall gave any indication of ownership or present use although the building is in fine condition and some recent modernisation has taken place to comply with access regulations. The windows are a tell tale sign that it was erected originally as a religious building.

stimulated by the process of supply and demand throughout the British Empire and colonies. The people associated with all this economic stimulation had to be housed and they required places to worship, eat and drink, be taken care of when ill, and these needs were met by the purveyors of corrugated iron buildings.

Religious influences within the upper classes were increasingly apparent during the nineteenth century and as some of the Evangelists found places in Parliament, they

St John's Church, Summerfield, near
Kidderminster

Standing in a delightful plot of land at the junction
of several roads, this church was dilapidated and
overgrown when photographed by the author in
2003. The sign had fallen down but the main
timberwork looked sound and although the
building had obviously been unused for some
time, structurally it looked as if it could be
brought back into use with little effort.

were in a position to bring about some radical social changes by the middle of the century. These radicals, mainly middle and upper class people, as the working classes still held no political power, were depicted at the time as sanctimonious do-gooders who were going to upset the status quo but their determination to bring about social change led to many changes which would benefit all classes of people.

These influences were also felt in Scotland where the revivals brought about the withdrawal in 1842 of 474 ministers from the Church of Scotland. They formed the Free Church of Scotland and within four years they collected enough money to build over 654 new churches. Non-conformity was also growing. In England and Wales the largest group, the Methodists, had grown from 72,000 in 1781 to over 385,000 by 1850. There were also 104,000 Primitive Methodists, 19,000 Wesleyan Methodists, 10,000 Christian Methodists and many of the other non-denominational sects probably did not declare themselves correctly in the censuses of the time because they remembered the religious persecutions of the previous century.

Corrugated Church, Swineford, Gloucestershire

This tin tabernacle on the A431 road between Bristol and Bath was apparently converted into a home at some time in its recent past. However it looks as if the occupiers may have moved on and it now looks in need of some tender loving care again.
Photos Phil Draper

Ex mission church at Streetly, West Midlands

This classic small corrugated church building
features tracery windows and ornate barge
boards. It stands in what appears to be quite a
rural position in the heart of the industrial
midlands on the side of a busy road. It is still in
use but the current owners run rather a
different business from the original occupiers
and it is now in use as the premises of a
printing and design company.

By the middle of the nineteenth century legislation was in place which prevented the exploitation of the working classes by regulating the number of hours which should be worked in the factories and mines. Education had improved and more of the population became literate. The publishing industry contributed to this with the number of newspapers, periodicals and books being published rising exponentially year by year. The Education Act of 1870 helped to ensure a basic education for all of the people.

However not everyone was to share immediately in the fruits of Britain's prosperity. Only one house in twelve had a water supply in Newcastle in 1846. Recurring cholera epidemics forced the central government to confront problems like the supply of clean water and the effective removal of sewage which had previously been left for the local authorities to deal with.

Further improvements began in the middle of the century. In 1851 the UK hosted the Great Exhibition – a celebration of all that was great about Britain – its economy, manufacturing prowess, and the moral example it set to the whole world. The huge pavilion erected using the latest architectural thinking and most modern materials showed Britain off as 'the workshop of the world'. The Crystal Palace as it was called by 'Punch' housed an astonishing array of produce, engineering, agriculture, buildings and art of every conceivable kind which showed the extent of economic prosperity in the country at that time. Up to 17 per cent of the British population came to view this 'eighth wonder of the world'. Britain was not only exporting produce, it was also investing huge amounts of money overseas in North America, Europe and its colonies abroad (over £700 million by 1870). By 1871 there were some 18,000 factories and workshops recorded in the metal manufacturing industry alone. Nearly half a million miners were employed and the output from the textile mills had doubled during the previous two decades. In 1856 steel production was improved with new techniques by Henry Bessemer and by 1870 annual

St Mary's Church, Woodland, Co Durham

At the beginning of the twentieth century services were held in the Woodland village school. However the people of Woodland wanted their own church and the money was raised to erect one. The church was built by voluntary labour. The communion and lectern were made and donated by local craftsmen. The church bell, like the lectern, was cast at Woodland Colliery 'back pit'. On January 17th, 1905, St Mary's was granted a licence for the performance of Divine Service and on the 21st the church was dedicated by the Bishop of Durham.
Photos Hilary Jackson

St Barnabus Church seen here in earlier days from a different angle.

St Barnabus Church, Darby Green, Diocese of Winchester
Photo Sandy Wright

Faversham Tin Church
(St Saviour's), corner of
Whitstable Road/Cyprus Hill,
Faversham, Kent

Then and now: the 1885 church
of St Saviours is still going strong
over a hundred years later. The
distinctive round window and bell
tower have not changed.

Photos Graham Goodwin

Chapel of Saint Vincente de Paul, Cambridge

This picturesque little Roman Catholic corrugated iron church was clad in wood when originally erected and is apparently only about 30 years old. The paint scheme is a tour de force of originality and the shuttered windows lend it a slightly mediterranean air which is perhaps appropriate for a Catholic church.
Photos Robin Lee

average production was 486,000 tonnes. To cope with the increasing population size, Britain had to import large quantities of food from abroad which it paid for with its manufacturing prowess, as well as its expertise in areas such as shipping, insurance and finance.

Throughout this intense period of industrialisation cities were growing in size. The middle classes looked towards the suburbs and commuting to work became the norm. In central London the mainline railway companies were attempting to build termini within the central region. This entailed wholesale clearance of housing which mostly affected the poor with some 50,000 losing their homes during the period. The major railways arrived in London during the 1860s with the Metropolitan opening the world's first underground railway (using steam trains!) in 1863. There were still enough commuters for the London General Omnibus Company to carry over 49 million passengers a year. Where the more affluent middle classes moved out to escape the incursion of railways and industry, the housing they left was often taken over by the very poor creating slum conditions and overcrowding.

During this period of social and moral upheavals, even the word of the Bible was subject to revision. This was entirely necessary based upon newly discovered texts which had come to light since the authorised version had been published under the rule of James I. In 1870 the Canterbury Convocation appointed a committee to revise and publish a new version which would include much new scholarship based on writing like the fourth century Codex Sinaiticus which had been discovered and studied on the continent. The new version of the Bible was published in 1881 but even this was regarded with suspicion in some quarters. However it did not produce the same reaction as some of the learned scientific publications of the time which appeared to be questioning the fundamental truths of the Bible upon which western society had based itself for nearly 2000 years. Studies by some of the early geologists and paleontologists seemed to

Seventh Day Baptist Church, Small Heath, Birmingham

This delightful urban church can be seen in the middle of Small
Heath on a busy road in the heart of Birmingham. It's a wonder
that this building has survived as so much of the local area has been
redeveloped and the building is surrounded on all sides by much
more modern brick and masonry structures. The church must have
a dedicated and loyal congregation.

show that other forms of life walked the earth well before man came along. When Charles Darwin published *The Origin of Species* in 1859 it questioned the foundations of the creation story in Genesis. Darwin followed this first book up with *The Descent of Man* in 1871 which gave rise to enormous problems for biblical scholars who now had to reconcile the scientific facts with the accepted word. In a debate at Oxford, Bishop Wilberforce famously enquired of Thomas Henry Huxley, a supporter of Darwin, whether he was descended from a monkey on his grandfather's side or his grandmother's.

The population of England and Wales in 1801 was more than 9 million (it stood at less than 6 million a century earlier in 1700). A fall in the death rate amongst infants and a propensity towards longer life combined with economic growth and improvements in agricultural techniques sustained this increasing population during the nineteenth century so that by 1851 the population had increased to 20 million. By 1871 another ten and a half million people had been added to the ever increasing total. The census of 1901 shows the population of the United Kingdom standing at well over 41 million. City populations had increased dramatically during this period as well; London had gone from a population of 1,117,000 in 1801 to 6,586,000 in 1901 and many other UK cities showed increases of up to 1000 per cent. This is even more remarkable when viewed against the numbers emigrating from the UK which rose steadily from as few as 2000 per year near the beginning of the nineteenth century to over a quarter of a million in 1882.

Improving education meant that by 1818 some 680,000 children were being educated at about 18,800 schools in England and Wales. There were also over 5,000 Sunday schools, some of which catered to adult groups as well as children. Scottish education at this time was generally better than in the rest of the country since the Scottish church had made provisions for a schoolmaster to serve each parish.

St Peter's Church Hall, Slough

The almost derelict church hall of St Peter's in Slough can be seen here looking not unlike a back street car mechanic's workshop.

Photos John Salmon

St Mary the Virgin, Shepperdine

A strange little tin church with bellcote and square windows which is open nearly all the time. Small porch at entrance. View from within is a bit like 'being in a ship' as one can see the fields with the river bank not far away. Very atmospheric – a couple of miles from Thornbury down a very narrow lane which goes almost to the river's edge. Must be one of the smallest churches in the country. Chapel House on the bank of the River Severn used to be the 'Chapel of St Mary on the Severn' and it existed before 1350 when Gilbert de Tyndene founded a Chantry (an endowment for a priest to celebrate mass for the founder's soul) consisting of a Saw Mill, 70 acres of land and 20 shillings of rent to maintain a Chapel to celebrate daily mass for the health of King Edward III and Gilbert himself. It is believed that the priest was also the lighthouse keeper. The lighthouse later became an ale house then a reading room for the sailor's on the Severn and it is now a house. The recently renovated present church is thought to have been used as a house by the son of one of the vicars. It was in the Parish of Rockhampton but is now in the Parish of Oldbury on Severn.

The rise of prefabricated corrugated iron building affected the whole of British architecture as the new materials took their place within the building and engineering industries. Britain's most forward thinking industries, the one associated with speed and movement, were the railway companies and it was these companies who first saw the potential of the new materials for building large structures very quickly and economically. As corrugated iron pervaded the industrial sector and was used increasingly in railway buildings by engineer-designers who could use it in ways and places where traditional materials would be either too expensive or simply not good enough, it was only a matter of time before some of the manufacturers and suppliers looked at other uses for the raw materials.

Iron churches were the perfect synthesis of industrial ability and social or spiritual need and they were advertised for nearly one hundred years as being the best solution to the problem of fast economic church building.

St Mary's Church, Burgh Parva, Norfolk

In the 1880s and '90s Melton Constable Village grew from virtually nothing to become the centre of the Midland and Great Northern Joint Railway. The M&GN was affectionately known as the Muddle and Get Nowhere and Melton was the junction for Cromer, Great Yarmouth, Norwich, Kings Lynn and Lt. Walsingham. In effect it was the 'Crewe' of North Norfolk.

The land on which the railway and the village were built had been owned by Lord Hastings. Part of the agreement with the railway company was that they should build a church for their workers on land given by Lord Hastings around the pre-1317 ancient ruined tower of Burgh Parva church. As a result a typical industrial solution was employed with the erection of a prefabricated church, made of corrugated iron, which became known as St. Mary's Burgh Parva. At one time the church boasted a good choir and it is still today used for worship, and now and again receives a coat of paint to smarten it up.

Constructed in 1903 by J Rolfe & Co, of Oswaldstre House, Norfolk Street, The Strand, London, Constructors of Iron Buildings. The cost was £272-12s-6d which included heating in the form of three Tortoise Slow Combustion Stoves. The building was intended to be temporary while funds were raised for the restoration of the more ancient structure alongside. Several other corrugated buildings can be found in this area, many lovingly restored by their owners.
Photos Gary Linder

St Mary's Chapel of Ease, Sawley, Derbyshire

This tin church was built in 1912 as a chapel to the mother church of All Saints, Sawley, following an expansion of population in an industrial district. The building was loaned for a period of 'six or seven years', but this seems to have been forgotten in the aftermath of the First World War. Apart from its uses as a place of worship, the following limitations were set out in the original deeds: No hotel, tavern, tea gardens, manufactory, mill, gas works, hospital, asylum, day school or shop, or any offensive, noisy or dangerous trade, business pursuit or occupation shall at any time be erected, opened or carried on and no spiritous or fermented liquors shall be sold in or upon any part of the said land or in any buildings erected thereon. The guillotine-like bell tower does not seem to deter its regular users.

St Nicholas Church, Severn Beach, near Bristol

Prior to 1930 this church may have been used elsewhere (one correspondent claimed it was built in the 1920s for less than £300 by public subscription). Quite a large structure, it has two ventilators on its roof, and a small porch with round window above. The building stands in its own little garden in the aptly named Church Road. Sadly this rather picturesque church has recently been demolished.

Christ Church Church Hall, Paignton

This iron church was built in the 1880s to serve as temporary accommodation
while the permanent stone building alongside was erected in 1888. After
completion of the much more grand permanent building it has been retained
and is still regularly used as a church hall.

Rodhuish Methodist Chapel (formerly
Bible Christian), Rodhuish, Somerset

Disused since the 1970s this charming
little church was built about 1898
presumably to serve the local
agricultural community. Some efforts
have been made recently to restore
the building and perhaps bring it back
into use as a community centre.

St Gabriels, Rough Common, near Canterbury, Kent

Little corrugated church with pantiled roof and bell tower under bracketed cover at front above porch. One might expect pantile or slate roofing to cause the roof timbers to buckle as the tiles are much heavier than the corrugated iron. However the original corrugated iron sheeting was of a much heavier gauge than we use today – sometimes as much as 6mm in thickness – so the roof timbers must have been designed to withstand this sort of weight.

Photos Graham Goodwin

Old Heath Congregational Church, Old Heath Road, Colchester, Essex built in 1869 and still in regular use by a loyal congregation. The building has an unusual roofline and is resplendent in its powder blue paintwork. It looks as if two buildings have been erected alongside each other but offset from each other and at an unusual angle to the road. This all adds to the charm and lends the building an exotic air.

Photo Maralyn Bambridge

Bramdean Common Church
(The Gypsy Church),
Bramdean Common,
Oxfordshire

This picturesque little tin
tabernacle stands hidden in
the woods of Bramdean
Common. Built in 1883 as a
'mission church to the gypsies
who camped in the woods at
this time', the church is still
used occasionally and the
annual ground rent of five
pence is still paid. See the early
postcard view on page 10.
Photos Mike Andrews

St John's Church Hall, Meadowfield, Co Durham

Plans for a parish hall were drawn up by the Glasgow firm of D Cowieson & Co.
The hall was built in 1909 beside St John's Church. The hall is T shaped and holds
over 400 people. It is well equipped with a stage, cloakroom, dressing rooms and
kitchen and is still used regularly by the local community.

St Columba's Mission Church, East Howle, Co Durham

St Columba's Mission Church was originally built to serve the growing colliery community at East Howle in 1901. Used since 1963 as agricultural storage, the building has acquired new roof and wall panels and the front has been fitted with large doors but the remains of the bell tower are still evident and the windows are a distinctive reminder of the building's original purpose. The old postcard view on page 16 gives a better idea of how imposing the church was originally.

Luckington Methodist Church, Luckington, near Chipping Sodbury.
Pity about the modern uPVC double glazed windows but at least the building is
probably warm in the winter and cool in the summer now.
Photo Phil Draper

St John's Chapel of Ease, Bellingdon, Chesham

Mr William Lowndes gave some land to the Vicar and
Church Wardens of St Mary's Church for the erection of
a Chapel or Mission Hall. The corrugated church was
bought as a prefabricated building for approximately
£100 and has been used ever since being erected in
1901. The vestry was added during the 1920s and
another extension to house a Sunday school was added
in the 1960s. Bellingdon Mission Church became St
John's Chapel of Ease and some stained glass windows
originally in the Liverpool Mission to Seamen were
incorporated at this time.

Photos: Marion Hall

Mission Church, Little Hay, Staffordshire

Another mission church on side of road in Little Hay photographed by the
author on a warm July afternoon. This one is painted in what seems to be one of
the most popular colours. It is probably just a co-incidence that the paint used
on these corrugated iron building very often resembles the paint colour used by
the incumbent local railway operator on their main line locomotives.

St Peter's Church, Lower Withington, Cheshire

Lee Bridges Methodist Church, Lee Bridges,
near Shrewsbury

The picturesque little corrugated Methodist
church seen here just as the sun goes down
features some interesting stained glass
lights high in the apex of the roof. The
carefully painted exterior and picket fence
indicate that this particular tin tabernacle
should enjoy quite a few more years life.

Bye Street Mission Hall, Bye Street, Ledbury

This former mission hall has been converted for use by a local funeral director which seems an entirely appropriate use for the building. It now features a brick built frontage which belies the corrugated construction behind. The exterior has been recently painted and appears to be in good condition. Perhaps 'well preserved' might be an appropriate description given its current use.

Abandoned tin mission at Knowle, Shropshire

This building is in stark contrast to the well kept church shown opposite which
is literally a few metres away on the same side of the road. No information
could be found about this building but one could suppose this was a rival
denomination which fell out of favour over the years.

The Knowle Mission, Knowle, Shropshire

This church is a mission church of St Peter's (Church of England), Parish of Coreley. Apart from a fairly mossy roof, it looks to be in reasonable condition and the notice board outside suggests that is used on a regular basis.

St Saviours Church, Westhouses, Derbyshire

This church was built for the Church of England in an area remote from the existing parish church where a new railway development had taken place. The building was erected by subscription and opened in 1898. After the building became redundant, it was dismantled and re-erected at the Midland Railway Centre, Swanwick, Derbyshire in 1997. Services are still occasionally held there.

Photo Keith Reedman reproduced courtesy of the Midland Railway Centre

Kemble Methodist Church, Kemble, Gloucestershire

The little Methodist Church at Kemble has obviously seen better days. The sign which should hang over the door has fallen onto the porch roof and, like many other tin tabernacles, the front windows look as if they have been sheeted over with corrugated iron. Whether this was to keep out prying eyes or for some other reason is open to conjecture.

Bethel Primitive Methodist Church, King Street, Long Eaton,
Derbyshire

The Primitive Methodist church, known as Bethel, was a tin
church in King Street, Long Eaton, built in 1898. The permanent
brick church, now a listed (Grade II) building was erected in
1904 (architect, George Baines, London) on an adjoining site.
The original tin church is still in use by the church.
Photo Keith Reedman

United Mission Church, Chapel Street, Long Eaton, Derbyshire

This tin church was originally a Railway Mission sited in Midland
Street, an area of Midland Railway housing. It was re-sited in
chapel Street after WWI to become the home of the United
Mission Church. It passed into secular use during the 1980s and
is now used for industrial purposes. The building is in a
Conservation Area.
Photos Keith Reedman

St John's Church, Granville Avenue, Long Eaton, Derbyshire

St John's mission was sited in one of the newer parts of the rapidly expanding town of Long Eaton in Derbyshire. The tin church was built in 1900 and continued in use as a hall by the church after a permanent building was erected in 1922. The tin church hall was destroyed by fire in April 1948 and this photograph of the event graphically illustrates how vulnerable these timber framed buildings are to fire. As long as there was nobody inside the building, the fire brigade would only be able to control the fire as there would be little hope of salvaging the building.

Collection of Michael Goy

St Michael & All Angel's Church, Junction of Stade Street and Portland Road, Hythe

A daughter church to St Leonard's Parish Church in Hythe built as mission to provide services for the working class families moving to the expanding area along the Royal Military Canal. The building was paid for by the vicar Reverend FT Scott and erected on land provided by the Watts family in 1893. The church was intended to seat about 280 people and furnished with an oak altar. The original gas lighting, coke stoves and manual organ were all replaced with their modern counterparts and some of the roof sheets have been 'modernised'. The church is still in regular use today.

Photos John Hendy

Albany Road Chapel, Newport, IoW

Church Hall in Southsea, Portsmouth

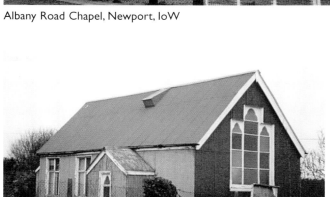

Chapel of St John, IoW

A miscellany of building from the Isle of Wight and Portsmouth area. Most of these buildings are gone now but the Chapel of St John (left) and the Mission Hall in Chale (below) are still in use.

Photos Catherine Taylor

Chapel of St Barnabus

Mission Hall, Chale, IoW

Former Moose Hall in Southsea, Portsmouth

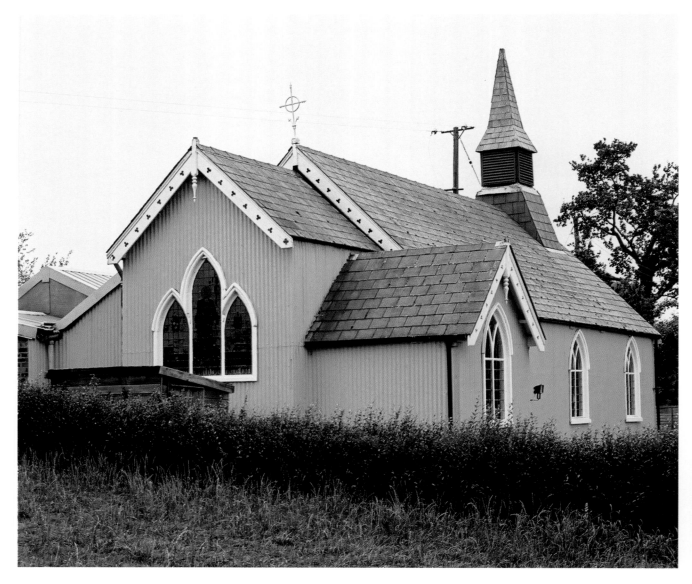

St Philip's Church, Hassall Green, near Haslington, Cheshire

Originally situated in the centre of Alsager, but removed when the permanent church of St Mary Magdalene was built in 1898. The local story is that a group of farmers saw it being dismantled, decided to adopt it, and rebuilt it on its present site. It can still be seen today in this stunning pink paintwork. The name of the supplier, Isaac Dixon of Liverpool, can be clearly seen on several plates attached to the walls, while a foundation stone near the main entrance door has the date 1888 carved into it.

Coombe Green Mission Hall nestling beside the Eastnor to Tewkesbury road at Coombe Green built c1887 and originally sited in nearby Hollybush. The roof was previously painted red which must have been quite attractive but now the whole building is the same colour. Apparently the church was erected under the direction of Lady Henry Somerset who felt that the incumbent Rector of Eastnor was less than welcoming to lower class church-goers. The good Lady took it upon herself to provide a place of worship where they would be made welcome.

Edithmead Mission Church, Parish of St Andrew, Burnham on Sea

This church was originally built as a schoolroom (which may explain the unusual
central 'spire') but it was moved to its present site in the corner of a field on
Edithmead Farm in 1919. Is well cared for and is used regularly.

St Columba Church, Catisfield

St Columba was opened in 1891 by William Thresher, a retired naval Commander, as a mission chapel of nearby Holy Trinity Church. 130 people attended the opening service. Enlarged in 1906 when a chancel was added. The building was sold in 1963 when it became the '106 Country Club' but this also closed in 1979. The building was eventually demolished in 1991 and these photographs taken during the demolition clearly show the timber framing common to all of these structures.

Photos by Doug Glading

St Augustine's Mission Church stands on a corner along the A515 in the countryside a few miles west of Burton upon Trent in the village of Draycott in the Clay, Staffordshire. With a well preserved bell tower, central ventilator and tiled roof, this is a very picturesque church in an equally picturesque scenic location. The tiles are artificial (probably asbestos) and were quite popular at one time on corrugated iron buildings. They were probably used in an attempt to make the building look less like a 'temporary' church.

Wesleyan Methodist Chapel, East Hedleyhope, Co Durham

This imposing church was built on the hill at the west side of the village of East Hedleyhope in 1892 as a Wesleyan Methodist Chapel. The chapel was originally sold in 1968 to a local football club for use as a clubhouse. It is currently used as a garage/workshop for large vehicles with the entire back end of the building replaced with sliding doors which are tall enough to allow buses and trucks to enter the building for work to be undertaken on them. The original foundation stones dating from 1893 can be seen on the corner to the right of the front door. Surrounded by woodlands and with a stream running alongside the road just opposite, its beautiful country location cannot be appreciated from the photographs but it must have been a delightful chapel to visit on a warm Sunday morning in its heyday.

Great Moulton Congregationalist Chapel, Museum of East Anglian Life,
Stowmarket

Resited 30 miles from its original home at Great Moulton, this 1890 church was
donated by its congregation when they built a new place of worship. Even the
total immersion font has been retained.

Photos Simon Knott reproduced courtesy of Museum of East Anglian Life, Stowmarket

Not much bigger than a domestic garage, one of the smallest tin churches in the country, the tiny Independent Baptist Church at Culkerton, Tetbury can be seen nestling in its idyllic rural environment in the larger photograph while another glimpse through the window in the smaller picture shows just how tiny the church is. There is a porch over the door which has been added since the church was originally built.

Mission Church near Crackenthorpe

This abandoned tin tabernacle was found on the side of the busy A66 road near Crackenthorpe. The church stands in its own little plot of land fenced off from the surrounding agricultural land. Very rusty and obviously unused for some time, the remains of a steeple or bell tower can be seen just behind the tree in the photograph. This church was probably built to cater for the spiritual needs of the local rural agricultural population as there do not seem to be any houses nearby.

Clows Top, near Kidderminster, Worcestershire

The Mission Room at Clows Top was 'built by parisioners and friends in memory of the late John Cawood, for 20 years Rector of Mamble and Bayton'. The local squire George Wickstead of Shakenhurst donated £10 to start subscriptions in 1895 and this church was dedicated on 22 October the same year. The MP father of Prime Minister Stanley Baldwin also contributed as did many others and the church was bought for £70-18s-0d. The Bishop's licence stipulated that the altar must be curtained off when the building was used for village tea parties (a common secondary use for these churches during temperance days). The paraffin lamps were replaced by electricity in 1948. The cleaning was undertaken in 1896 by Mr Millward who was paid 12/6 twice a year for this service. In 1919 many years later he was still paid the same 12/6 which is about 52p in modern currency.

All Saints Church, Brokerswood, Dilton Marsh, near Westbury, Wiltshire

The little tin church at Brokerswood was erected on its current site in 1904 but was previously at Southwick.

St Andrew's Church, Button Oak, near Bewdley, Worcestershire

St Andrew's Church, Button Oak built in 1873 was originally the daughter church of Dawles parish church and was built on land given by Robert Woodward of Arley Castle. C. Pounteny of Bewdley is recorded as the builder of the foundations and the contractor/supplier responsible for the erection of the church was S Dyer (Iron Church Builder of Euston Road, London). Dawles and Button Oak were in the Hereford Diocese but in 1940 the parish became part of the united benefice of Ribbesford with Bewdley and Dawles in the diocese of Worcester.

The Church underwent a dedicated restoration and refurbishment in 1975 which saw the addition of a kitchen, cloak room and toilet facilities. At this time the exterior corrugated cladding was replaced with cedar panelling but this has not changed the outward appearance of the church greatly – it is still immediately recognisable as a 'tin tabernacle' (perhaps 'timber tabernacle' might be more appropriate). The roof has also been repaired recently along with some of the windows including the blue glass which was added to the sanctuary window.

St Michael's Church, Breadstone, Berkley,
near Bristol

Built in 1878 but sadly unused for a
number of years, the interior of the
church at Breadstone, glimpsed through a
window above, shows the church fittings
still in place and almost ready (apart from
the dust) to be used again.

Bridgetown Village Hall, Bridgetown, Somerset

Former asylum hospital set on steep hillside just beside the A396 road. Corrugated iron structures were offered as quick solutions to many building problems and during the 1800s when epidemic diseases were still a common threat to life in the UK, quite a few hospitals were built in rural areas so that patients could be segregated from the rest of society where they could recover with less risk of spreading contagious infections further.

Bridge Methodist Church, Bridge, near Canterbury

A very simple but elegant building still in regular use. The toplights over the arched door have been retained but some of the other windows have been less sympathetically replaced.

Photo courtesy of John & Andrew Wittich Photographic Collection ©

This corrugated iron hall was last used as a campaign headquarters by the local Labour party but it does not look like it will be in use for much longer.

Birdwood Mission Church, Birdwood, west of Gloucester

Situated alongside the A40 road between Cheltenham and Gloucester, the Birdwood Mission Church is a strange mixture of ecclesiastical and industrial. The windows on the road side of the building are simple square units while some of the windows which face out into the surrounding fields have a more obviously ecclesiastic appearance. The ornate but spindly bell tower invokes a certain Swiss elegance.

St Chads Mission, Ironbridge Gorge Museum, Telford, Shropshire

Built in 1888 to serve the colliers in the industrial area around Granville Mine near Telford. The building was bought as a mail order kit from a company in London for about £120. It is still a consecrated church and is used for occasional services including Victorian style weddings. It is also used occasionally by television and film companies as a setting for period drama pieces. The church features an unusual pagoda style roof – perhaps the last one in existence as most tin churches have flat-surfaced roofs. This pagoda style roofing was used by the Great Western Railway on some of its corrugated iron buildings and adds a slightly oriental air to the building. The gravestones seen next to the church are, perhaps surprisingly, also made out of iron.

Picture reproduced courtesy of the Ironbridge Gorge Museum

St Felix Chapel, Babingley
On the royal estate in Norfolk

Circa 1300, a church dedicated to St Felix was built in the village of Babingley, just north of Castle Rising near Kings Lynn. The village became depopulated, and by 1895 the church was abandoned, having already been shortened. Nothing remains of the village and the original church is now a ruin.

The site is part of the Sandringham royal estate. In 1894-1895 the then Prince of Wales built the iron church shown here with its unusual (but not unique) thatched roof. It too, was dedicated to St Felix. It became disused, and the Diocese of Ely disposed of it. In the nineteen seventies, a tree fell on to it and knocked part of the roof off.

However the story does have a happy ending – the British orthodox church took it on. They asked HM The Queen if they could use it, and she said yes. They spent £20,000 re-thatching the roof and it is now back in regular use.
Photos John Salmon

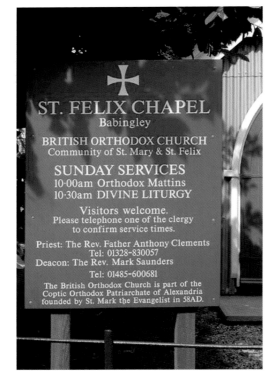

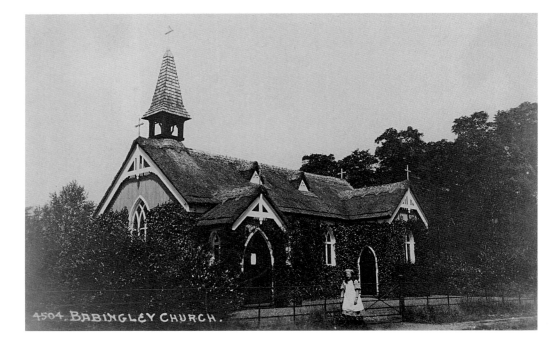

Bilson Mission, Cinderford, Gloucestershire

The mission church of St Stephen's is a plain building which features a very interesting bell turret which looks rather like a bird house perched on top of its pole at one end of the roof. Its dedicated congregation use it regularly for worship as well as for a variety of community based activities.

This unassuming little shed, not much bigger than an average family garage, is actually St Patrick's Church in Alsager, Cheshire. Now looking slightly the worse for it years, this building is still obviously used by its congregation and although the paintwork is not as adventurous as that seen on some corrugated iron churches, at least the paint has been quite recently applied.

Bringsty Iron Church 1891, now at the Avoncroft Museum of Historic Buildings

This 12 metre long church building was supplied from a catalogue by JC Humphrey's Iron Yards and Works of Ludgate Station, London. Dismantled and then re-erected at Avoncroft Museum of Historic Buildings in Herefordshire forty miles from its original site at Bringsty. The museum curator said at the time 'It represents an historic moment in architectural design – the introduction of corrugated iron as a new, durable building material. It is a perfect example of buildings which were once numerous all over the world'.

Picture reproduced courtesy of the Avoncroft Museum of Historic Buildings

Exterior of
Alhampton Church
near Ditcheat built in
1892

Architect George
Chedburn, who was
commissioned to assess
the state of repair of
the church at
Alhampton stated 'We
recently opened up the
structure to investigate
the condition of the
timber frame,
anticipating that we
would find a large
number of major
defects. However, to
our surprise, we found
that the structure is in
remarkably good
condition and any
defects are fairly easy
to repair. In addition,
the galvanising on the
tin cladding fixings has
remained remarkably
intact...'

Little information could be found about this disused corrugated iron church situated in the heart of a conglomeration of housing in Alma Road, Enfield. The building will probably have been demolished by the time this book is published.

Photo John Salmon

St John's Church, Adlington, daughter church of nearby St Peter's in the diocese of Chester, is in Brookledge Lane, and serves the Adlington end of the parish. Erected as a prefabricated temporary church in 1892 and still in regular use. Photographed by the author on a hot summer day, the overhead electricity lines which cross directly over the church were crackling loudly which added a very ominous and uncomfortable feeling to the location.

The truncated spire of this rather grand old iron church in Cambridge Avenue, Kilburn, London tells part of the story of its demise. This is a very large tin tabernacle, originally St James Episcopalian (Free) Church and when it was built c1863, it must have given some of the other more established churches a good run for their money if the congregation numbers were as big as the church was capable of holding. Now in a very sorry state, efforts are currently underway to restore the building for community use. The whole structure is sitting on concrete pillars with no proper foundations and was obviously only ever meant to be temporary. It is a minor miracle that a building like this has survived for so long in central London outlasting two wars and several building development booms. It is currently referred to as Cambridge Hall and was last home to the Willesden & St Marylebone Sea Cadet Corps.

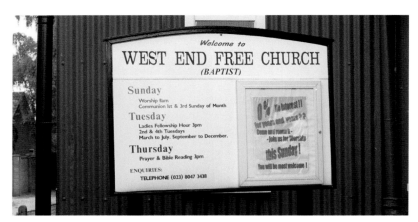

West End Free Baptist Church, near Southampton

The roof of this church features several ventilators and the truncated remains of a bell tower can be seen on the nearest end.
Photos Gwyn Powell

Woodcote House School Chapel, Windlesham, Surrey

The corrugated iron chapel at Woodcote House School was built sometime between 1834 and 1865 as a Family Chapel when the land was owned by the Pears family, one of whom decided to turn the estate back into a school (prior to 1834 it had been an Academy for the children of the Gentlemen of Sandhurst). The Chapel has some very fine stained glass windows dated 1878 including this copy of the famous Holman Hunt painting. The Chapel is used regularly for two weekly services; one for the school assembly on Wednesday morning and another on Sunday for the boarders and some of their parents. The original organ now houses more modern workings but the surrounding case sports hundreds of initials carved into it over the years by schoolboys who had been relegated to 'pumping' duty after their voices broke.

Photo Nick Paterson, Headmaster

Bethel Baptist Chapel, Chignall St James (above)

Quite a late building of 1926, this little corrugated chapel
is still in regular use.
Photo Rosalind Kaye

Right: this very attractive colour tinted postcard from
c1906 illustrates the delightful little church of St Andrew
at Sharpness. The extremely businesslike telegraph pole
on the right contrasts well with the flagpole seen on the
left. The rather stern deacon does not appear to be
enjoying the photographic session.

Bailbrook Mission Church, Bath

The Grade 2 listed church from 1892 set in the hills above Bath is noted as 'an exceptionally elaborate example'. Bought from the catalogue of William Cooper, Horticultural Providers, of 752 Old Kent Road, London by the good people of Bailbrook in an effort to bring the good word to the locals who worked in the nearby Robertson's jam orchards and had a reputation for gambling and drunkenness.

Its owner, who bought the church from the last vicar for £1500 cash, is in the process of restoring the church to its former glory where he will be able to live and work. One of the more recent modifications is the space-age lifting roof section which is used occasionally for festive occasions.

Photos Graham Boys/John Severne

Christ Church, Pointon

Christ Church, Pointon is situated in the village near the church school.
Commonly known locally as 'The Mission', 'The Winter Church' or just 'The Iron
Church' it was built from a kit supplied by the predecessor of the Incorporated
Church Building Society in about 1892. The intention, as usual, was to replace it
with a permanent building but this never happened. Christ Church was given by
Queen Victoria (there is a large Crown estate locally). It is still used and holds a
license for weddings.
Photo Christopher Wilson

This unusual view shows the rear of the mission church of St Phillip at Adlington,
Lancashire.

A superb colour tinted postcard view of the
impressive Baptist Chapel at Seven Kings from
the early twentieth century. The church hall or
Sunday School room can be seen behind the
main church building and advertising placards
surround the church – even the house next
door has signs advertising Nestles Milk on the
upper part of its wall.

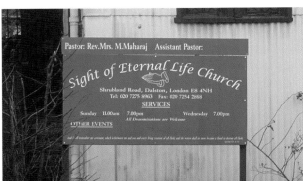

The Grade II listed tin church in Shrubland Road, Dalston, London is quite an early survivor having apparently been built in 1858. It does look a little dilapidated now but at least it has retained its rather distinctive spire and original windows which have an unusual triangular-pointed gothic shape.

St John's Christian Spiritualist Church, Finchley, London

This well hidden corrugated iron building has been used by the same church group since 1932. It was probably erected at this site around 1920 and was previously used as a school. It is standard construction timber framing with corrugated iron exterior and timber panelled interior. The elaborate stained glass windows have been provided over the years by subscriptions from church members or their families.

Photos Michael A Stanway/Author

The Bible Truth Church of God, Hetherington Road, Brixton, London

This lovely old traditional tin tabernacle is tucked down a small road in Brixton where it sits right next to the newer community centre and contrasts strikingly with some of the buildings nearby. It has been carefully looked after over the years and, judging by the on-going repairs being carried out when the author visited, it will probably still be going strong in another hundred years.

Castle Sowerby Chapel, Castle Sowerby, Yorkshire

This Free Evangelical Chapel in Castle Sowerby is in very good condition. Apart from the slightly mossy roof it looks like it has just been built.

Photos Andrew Smith

'Holly Lodge' Church, Ipswich

Photo D Kensick

The Sunday School Annexe, Liss
Evangelical Church, Liss, Hampshire

This little corrugated iron building was
under threat of demolition at the time
the photograph was taken.
Photo Colin Dring

Women's Institute Hall, Yorkshire

This large building was probably a school or mission hall originally.

Photos Andrew Smith

Ex Mission Hall, Durley, Hampshire

Now used as a children's play centre, this corrugated iron building on the
outskirts of the old village of Durley has an unusual lean-to outbuilding with a
very tall brick built chimney stack protruding from its roof. The double windows
over the front entrance porch are also quite a departure from standard practice.
The hook at one end of the roof must have some purpose?

Photos Christopher Powell

Woodmancote, Emsworth, Hants

Erected by Rector Dr Mee in 1892 to be used for 'any meeting or other objects
having in view the spiritual, intellectual, moral or social wants of professing members
of the Church of England'. Still conducts services announced by the ringing of the
little green bell above the porch and accompanied by a harmonium.
Photo Gwyn Powell

Meeting Room, Defford, Worcestershire

On the A4104 just south of Pershore stands this little Meeting Room or
Brethren Chapel built in about 1893. Neatly maintained and still in use.
Photos David Taylor/Caroline Adey

Church Hall, Boldmere Road, Sutton Coldfield

In the middle of the developed urban areas
the West Midlands one can still see a
surprising number of corrugated iron halls
like this one photographed in November
2003 which stands between the church and
the post office. Its current use is unknown
but the burglar alarm, refurbished windows
and expensive cars parked outside leads one
to speculate whether it is being used as a
light industrial unit or for some other
business purposes.
Photos David Taylor/Caroline Adey

St Georges Barracks, Fort Rowner, Gosport, Hants

In 1919 this place in Gosport – then known as New Barracks – provided home for one of the battalions making up the peacetime Solent Garrison (9th Infantry Bde) – deemed necessary for the protection of Portsmouth and its naval installations; others being stationed in Portsmouth, Parkhurst and Weymouth. Built around the same time, the barrack's tin church has seen better days but the whole barracks area is currently being redeveloped and the church will be restored and made use of in some way. The bicycle standing next to the door seems to be a poignant reminder of the past.

Photos Christopher Powell

United Reformed Church, Sealand Road, Whipcord Lane, Chester

The corrugated iron church built about 1909 seen here in Chester is
overshadowed by the tree growing in its garden on the corner. The roof has
been replaced with modern box section corrugated sheeting but most of
the original features like the roof ventilators and cast iron crosses have
been tastefully retained.

Chapter 4

SCOTLAND

Over the next few pages you will be able to see a variety of iron churches and halls, most of which are still standing in Scotland. The examples pictured here are a far-from-exhaustive snapshot of those that are waiting to be discovered and Scotland seems to be the most forward thinking on a local level when it comes to preserving these little buildings for use as community assets. Indeed some of the corrugated iron buildings that can be found in Scotland are so enormous and the surrounding communities so small that one begins to wonder who makes use of these buildings.

Postcard collection of Muriel Steer

MOFFAT. St. John's Episcopal Church. Situated on Millburn-side. Erected in 1872 by the late J. T. Lawrence, Esq., a Liverpool Merchant, long resident in Craigieburn House. The Church is very comfortable and has a fine Organ. The Rector is the Rev. John Molony, B.A.
'Annandale' Series. J. Weir, Photo., Moffat.

St John's Episcopal Church,
Moffat, Scotland

Kinbrace Mission, Kinbrace, Highlands

Photographed on a bleak summer day in the Scottish Highlands, the mission hall
at Kinbrace urgently needs some fresh paint and looks like it is rarely used. The
delightfully dilapidated picket fence which surrounds the building is unlikely to
keep out any of the animal visitors which it was erected to deter.

Corrugated Hall, Onich, Scottish Highlands

This large corrugated hall on the edge of the A482 road at Onich offers no outward indication of its original purpose. Perhaps it was originally a school house as the chimney implies that it was properly heated by a fire at some time in the past.

Portsonachan Church, Portsonachan, South side of Loch Awe, Scottish Highlands

The Parish of Glenorchy and Innishail has a nice little tin tabernacle dating from the early 1900s in the middle of the village of Portsonachan. Photographed in July 2003 the church needed some internal repairs as part of the ceiling was falling down and the roof space had been used by birds for nesting inside. The building sits on sturdy foundations alongside the Loch and several other corrugated iron structures, including houses, can also be found in the village.

United Free 'Tin' Church, Isle of Seil, Slate Islands, Scotland

This large building is located about 15 miles south of Oban on the B844 just before Seil which used to be centre of the Scottish Slate industry. The church was apparently being used for agricultural storage at the time it was photographed. It is extremely similar in design to the church at Elphin although the Elphin building appears to have had the skylight over the door frame boarded over. This church is situated in a very rural part of Scotland and the congregation must have had quite a journey to get to it on Sundays but apparently it was not uncommon for people to spend all day at or around the church socialising as well as worshipping, so perhaps the journey was worthwhile.

St Fillan's Church, Killin, Stirlingshire, Scotland

White walls and a green roof make this little Scottish Episcopal church a prominent feature in the main street of Killin. The inside is beautifully finished in red pine and the church is dedicated to Saint Fillan, an Irish saint with a reputation for healing who lived in the area in the ninth century. It was almost certainly bought from the Glasgow manufacturer Spiers & Co and erected c1876. The window frames are similar to those on the church in Fort Augustus.

Syre, Highlands, Scotland

The corrugated iron church at Syre was built as a mission church by the Free Church of Scotland in 1891 to serve the agricultural community of the Sutherland Estate. The church has twice changed allegiance – in 1900 the congregation voted to join with the United Presbyterian Church to form the United Free Church which in 1929 joined the mainstream Church of Scotland. This is a well preserved tin church in a beautiful location, with the door always open for visitors and the interior probably almost unchanged since the church was built. An information panel opposite tells the history of the church and its surrounding community while an illustration on the panel shows the massive corrugated iron agricultural building which used to stand behind the church.

Tomatin Church, Tomatin, Scottish Highlands

The corrugated iron Church of Scotland at Tomatin was built c1910 and is still in
regular use. The builder at the top of the ladder just behind the pulpit is
undertaking some minor internal repairs after a small fire damaged the interior
wall panels.

Church Hall, Killin, Stirlingshire, Scotland

Killin has a number of corrugated buildings including the church hall seen above and this delightful little bakery (right). There is also the iron church of St Fillans illustrated elsewhere in this work which is a more typical 'tin temple' as they are sometimes referred to in Scotland.

The Millshop, Fort Augustus, Highlands, Scotland

Old tin tabernacle converted to retail use as The Mill Shop selling highland gifts
in this popular stopping point for tourists visiting the Lochs of Scotland. The
building is in excellent condition internally and externally and the pointed
windows have been modernised quite tastefully. The bell tower survives in good
condition and the octagonal window over the entrance porch is an unusual
feature. Unfortunately the shop staff did not know anything about the history of
the building.

Leanach Church, Highland Folk Museum, Newtonmore

These photographs show the interior and exterior of the preserved Leanach Church at the Highland Folk Museum. This building was dismantled and moved from its original location to become one of the key exhibits at the museum which also has a preserved corrugated iron school house. While the exterior is a slightly unusual shape, the interior is typical of this type of building and clearly shows the simple tongue and groove wall cladding and interior decor as well as the structural members holding up the roof which have been supported with metal cross bracing to stop the building twisting and warping (a common fate of these prefabricated structures).

Picture reproduced courtesy of the The Highland Folk Museum, Newtonmore, The Highland Council

Disused Hall, Duror, Highlands, Scotland

This grey hall on the A482 north of Duror looked as if it had not been used for
quite a few years although the paintwork was in remarkable condition and it sits
on sound foundations. It also seemed to be situated as far away as possible from
any pockets of population. There are no obvious clues about its former use – it
may have been a school house or mission church.

Iron School House, Highland Folk Museum, Kingussie & Newtonmore

This corrugated building was dismantled and moved from its original location to join the preserved corrugated iron church which the Highland Folk Museum also features. Buildings of this type are quite common in Scotland and many have been retained for use as community halls.

Picture reproduced courtesy of the The Highland Folk Museum, Newtonmore, The Highland Council

Dalswinton Mission, Dumfries & Galloway, Scotland

This large corrugated iron mission church was built in 1881. It features gothic
windows and a steeply spired east bellcote. The interior is timber lined with an
open roof and chancel formed between a vestry and the laird's pew at the west
end. There is a modern semi abstract stained glass west window illustrating
scenes in the life of King David created by Cyril Wilson and added in 1975. The
north wall has an earlier and more representational stained glass scene created
and installed about 1950.

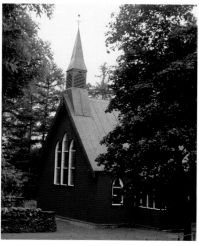

The 'Old Tin Church', Dulnain, Highlands, Scotland

This is a very attractive little tin church in a 'picture book' setting in the Scottish Highlands. In its woodland setting in a valley surrounded on all sides by steep mountains, it features an attractive timber porch which appears to be a later addition as the main part of the building looks like a standard off the shelf iron church. Most of these buildings have a very simple corrugated iron porch – this is probably the only one with such an ornately constructed and glazed entrance.

St Mary the Virgin Episcopal Church, Connel, Argyle & Bute

This little structure has been described as a 'corrugated iron shed with half-timber aspirations. Openings have moulded hoods with shaped pelmet facings'. This type of external timber work which does add a pseudo-Elizabethan feeling to the building is not so unusual in Scottish corrugated iron churches. This example is quite small and has now been converted for use as a shop trading (when photographed) as 'Keltia' selling celtic arts and crafts which seems an entirely appropriate use for such a picturesque building.

Contin Village Hall, Contin, Highlands

Yet another massive corrugated iron hall in the Scottish Highlands. The white village hall at Contin features black trim, red curtains and a very rusty roof seen here under a typical lowering Scottish sky.

Carrutherstown Hall, Carrutherstown, Dumfries

The town hall at end of the small village of Carrutherstown on the A75 in
Scotland. The village has only a small number of houses and is surrounded by
countryside so one wonders if this was not originally a mission church although
the windows and door are perhaps plainer than would normally be found in an
ecclesiastic building.

Closeburn Village Hall, Closeburn, Dumfries

Scotland seems to have more than it fair share of large corrugated iron halls.
This one at Closeburn is quite a substantial building which has been extended
over the years and it is still the focal point of community life. The roof
ventilators would not be out of place over a railway engine shed but the delicate
weather vane contrasts well with the massive unfussy end of the building.

Bridge of Dee Mission School, Bridge of Dee, Dumfries

This extremely attractive little corrugated iron school house was built in 1897.
Note the extra timber work under the porch roof – perhaps to shelter the
children a little more from the elements as they waited for the school to open
on a winter morning? It is a pity about about the corrugated transparent plastic
sheeting covering the windows but at least it protects the original window
frames and adds a crude double glazing to the building.

St Columba's Scottish Episcopal Church, Brora, Scottish Highlands

Large Hall, Portgower, Highlands

This large hall built on a sloping site near the sea at Portgower on the eastern coast of Scotland seemed to be still in regular use when visited, but there was no outside evidence to indicate what it was used for.

Our Lady of Mercy, Aberfeldy, Perthshire

Built in 1885, at the time of writing this church was under threat of demolition despite being a listed building. The Architectural Heritage Society of Scotland considers the church to be 'an important part of the architectural heritage of Aberfeldy'. Apart from the missing bell tower it looked externally to be in a fair state of repair and the ornate iron ridge castings and decorative timber eaves certainly add to its charm as it nestles among the houses in a side street in Aberfeldy.

Church of Scotland, Elphin, Highlands

When photographed in 2003 the
church has a notice pinned to its
front door stating that it is
condemned as dangerous by the local
council building department. This is
quite a large building – the ceiling
must be very high and judging from
the small high window placement it
must also have been quite dark
inside. There was probably another
skylight above the door which has
been blanked off with some plywood.

Chapter 5

WALES

St Thomas (Church in Wales), Trethomas, Rhondda, South Wales

Quite large corrugated iron building, next to the school in Trethomas. Painted green with high windows and a large bell tower.

Wales has been referred to in the past as the land with 'hundreds of tin tabernacles'. During the heydays of the great religious revivals this may have been true but sadly there are few good examples left in Wales. Most of those that can be found are rather small and any ornate decorations that they may have enjoyed early on in their lives have disappeared over the intervening years. Some of the remaining Welsh iron churches have been recognised for their architectural importance and others that remain are often situated in gritty industrial locations or beautiful rural ones.

WOODFIELD CHURCH PONTLLANFRAITH.

Right: long since demolished, this rather typically Welsh view showing mountains, grazing sheep and farm buildings also features the steeply roofed iron church at Woodfield, Pontllanfraith in Monmouthshire. This church seems to have a brick built chimney alongside instead of the more usual metal chimney.

Halton Former Mission Church,
Halton, Wrexham

This listed mission church built in 1878
has been bought and beautifully
refurbished as a home. Because of its
listed status it has been fully restored
to its former appearance with new
windows and new corrugated cladding.
When first spotted the cladding was in
its 'raw' galvanised state so the church
looked like a chrome plated beacon of
light in the rural landscape, especially
when compared to the well-known fast
food restaurant at the top of the hill
nearby. Now that the building has been
painted in its original cream and dark
green it looks more like a traditional
church building but closer inspection
reveals the attention to detail and the
care which has been lavished upon its
restoration.

'Red Pisgah' Mission, Cilffriw, Neath, West Glamorgan, Wales

This tin tabernacle was originally sited at nearby Seven Sisters. Dismantled and brought to Cilffriw, allegedly by river which seems unlikely, more probably by train. In 1890 there was a violent storm in the area which resulted in heavy floods engulfing the village of Cilffriw. It is said that the Minister prayed for salvation and then, by some miracle, the prayers were answered as a large boulder dislodged by the rushing torrent of water approaching the chapel, diverted the water away from the building and saved the chapel from being washed away. The women of Cilffriw are said to have carried stones in their ffedogs (aprons) to build the foundation for Pisgah Vestry.

Knolton Mission Church, Knolton Bryn, Overton, Wrexham

Grade 2 listed building, daughter church to St Mary's set up by Rev GJ Howson c1887 to help local people avoid the journey to the mother church St Mary's. There was some talk of dismantling the church and re-erecting it at the Museum of Welsh Life, St Fagans in South Wales but local protest has so far allowed the community to retain their tin church.

Llanddewi Skirrid Village Hall, Near Abergavenny, Wales

This mission hall was built originally to cater for the spiritual needs of the workmen and families constructing a reservoir near Abergavenny, possibly near Talybont on Usk. After a period as a church on this site it was bought and transported to its current location by Crawshay Bailey Junior, only son of the iron master, coal industry pioneer and railway entrepreneur, who paid for its re-erection as an Assembly room and Sunday school for the village of Llanddewi Skirrid about 1885.

The hall was listed Grade 2 in 1998 as a scarce example of a well-designed and unaltered late nineteenth century pre-fabricated iron church hall.

The building is standard corrugated iron sheets on timber construction, mostly original although the roof has been replaced at some time. The nave, transept and south porch have a Gothic flavour. The entrance elevation has a steeply gabled porch with scalloped bargeboards and a double planked door in a pointed arch. There are three 2-light windows with narrow mullions and transom with Gothic heads. A larger 3-light window with two mullions is in the transept gable with a smaller single one above. Two similar 2-light windows can be found in the gable end with the opposite gable having a small fleche shaped window in the gable apex.

The hall is still used regularly for village and church events including an Annual Fete and Show in September.

Hall at Llansteffan, Carmarthenshire, Wales

Quite a large tin chapel on the main road through Llansteffan in the Tywi Estuary south of Carmarthen. The building date is unknown but the chapel is shown on a map of 1891 as an Independent Chapel. Sited on a small piece of land with reasonably ornate iron railings and double gates to the front, it survives as a storage shed filled with various pieces of timber and other building materials.

St David's Church Hall, Llwynhendy, Llanelli, Wales

Very dilapidated church hall across the busy road from the main church. It had a felt or fibre 'slate' roof. Recently demolished.

St John the Baptist Church, Maesbury, near Oswestry

Built in 1906 on land given by the Lloyd family of Aston Hall (about 2 miles from the church). The church arrived in kit form on the back of a wagon and was erected by two men on foundations which had been prepared earlier. The church was a mission or daughter church to Holy Trinity, Oswestry for many years and it was served by the clergy from there. Originally licensed only for baptisms and funerals, the church was licensed for weddings in 1994. St John's church was transferred to the parish of Kinnerley and then in 1996 it became an independent parish with its own priest-in-charge.

Mission Hall, Nantgwynant, Gwynedd, Wales

Green mission hall set in a lush valley adjacent to abandoned Post Office and other buildings. The small glimpse through the window (below) shows the old harmonium still in place alongside the hearth of the pot belly stove which now has a disconcertingly modern chair standing upon it.

Eglwys Dewi Sant
(St David's Church), Nebo,
near Aberaeron, Wales

Unusually this church at Nebo built
in 1913 is sited in a field large enough
to also house a cemetery and a
second corrugated iron building
which is used as a church hall for
events and meetings.

St Anne's, New Hedges, near Tenby, Wales

Quite a modern tin church erected in 1928 holds a congregation of just 50 'at a push'. Fully restored in 2001 and painted a beautiful blue. The church features a bell and some very exotic cast ironwork along the roof ridges.

St Clement's Church Hall, Neyland, Pembrokeshire

A large church hall in the centre of Neyland, much of it now clad in shiplap
timber replacing earlier corrugated ironwork. Painted almost pillar box red, it
stands next to the much larger stone church building erected in 1930, which was
probably built to replace the iron structure.

Imposing corrugated hall with slated roof north of Clyndwerwen built in 1928.

Church Hall, Pembroke Dock, Pembrokeshire

This large hall was probably bought from one of the many military establishments around Pembroke Dock and relocated in its present position. The corrugated sheeting has a more modern and substantial profile than the earlier Victorian material.

Pembroke Apostolic Church, Pembroke, Wales

Built in 1913 by Plymouth Brethren coming to work in Pembroke Dock yard
from Portsmouth/Plymouth. The money needed was raised locally. The dockyard
in Pembroke Dock closed about 1926 and the building was taken over by the
Apostolic Church whose headquarters are in Penygroes, Carmarthen. The
foundation stones are still visible to the right of the entrance porch and the one
shown here reads 'This stone was laid by John Grieve Esq Mayor of Pembroke,
1913'.

Pendoylan War Memorial Hall, Pendoylan, South Wales

This grand iron hall has been 'modernised' recently with the original cladding being replaced with modern box section steel. If the porch and decorative external timbers were removed it could alomost pass for the kind of modern light industrial unit one expects to see in a more urban setting.

St Anne's Church, Penllergaer, Swansea

Another recently refurbished and lovingly cared for tin tabernacle. This one is in Penllergaer near Swansea and is distinguished by being set in a very large plot of land with a park behind. Perhaps the land was originally purchased or donated with the intention of building a much larger and more permanent church than the 'temporary' iron church which is still standing.

Memorial Hall, Pumsaint, Carmarthenshire

This building, one of the largest in the rural village of Pumsaint in West Wales has recently been treated to some much needed restoration work. Some of the other buildings are also clad in corrugated iron and the nearby National Trust owned Dolaucothi Gold Mine has many old corrugated iron buildings including one which houses a superb visitor centre which tells the largely unknown story of gold mining in this part of the world.

Tin building in Pwllglas, North Wales

No indication of its original use could be seen when it was photographed. It is built on the side of a steep hill along the main road. All the windows along the side of the building nearest the road have been sheeted over and the remaining windows had blinds or curtains to keep prying eyes out.

Bethel Evangelical Church, Rhoose, Wales

This unassuming little structure is the second iron hall in the village of Rhoose. It
was erected in 1904 as Pentecostal/Apostolic but is now an Evangelical Church.
As well as regular Sunday worship it also hosts a Sunday school, weekday prayer
meetings, bible study groups and a youth club.

St Peter's Church Hall, Rhoose, South Wales

Traditional little tin church hall standing next to the more permanent stone church. The early postcard view above shows the tin church which this hall was built alongside which was replaced by a stone building. The postcard clearly shows the church hall which still stands even though the main tin church has been replaced.

A very large and imposing corrugated hall near Pontypridd, South Wales

Ystrad Fechan Gospel Hall, Ystrad Fechan, Rhondda, Wales

Another busy Gospel Hall managing three meetings on Sundays and a mid week meeting for prayer and bible study.

Church of St Andrew, The Wern, Minera, Wrexham

This large church is situated in a rural area near Wrexham in north Wales. It was built in 1882 and still used regularly. It has been listed by Cadw (Welsh Historic Monuments) as a building of significant historic importance. The main part of the roof has been replaced with a more modern steel sheet material but the windows, eaves, some of the cast roof ridges and most of the side cladding is original.

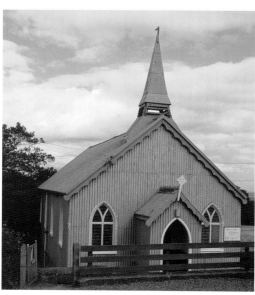

Seventh Day Adventist Church, Trealaw, Rhondda, Wales

This tumble down building situated on the edge of a very steep hill in the mining valleys of South Wales was bought from Trealaw Council c1922. Used to be Council Offices.

United Reformed Church, Tredomen, Powys

Very attractive little chapel which is set in a beautiful garden overlooking the
Brecon Beacons.

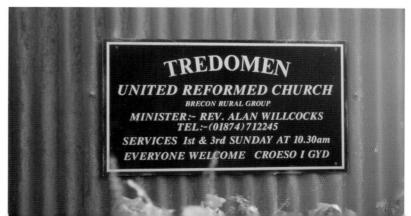

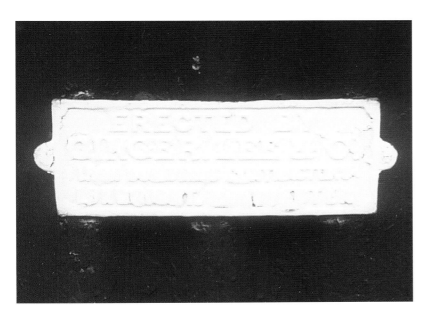

Hall near Forden, Powys, Wales

Standing alongside the Ebenezer Congregational Church on the side of the A490 near Forden north of Montgomery, this corrugated iron hall is in good condition and still has the original manufacturer's plate attached. The inscription on the plate reads 'Erected by Ginger, Lee & Co. Iron Building Constructors', the last line is probably the manufacturer's address but it has been obscured by decades of paint.

Photos Carolyn Adey & David Taylor

Community Hall, Ystrad, Rhondda, South Wales

This large corrugated iron building is now used as the Ystrad Old Age Centre.

St Andrew's Mission Church, Beaufort Hill, Ebbw Vale, South Wales

Built in 1898 as a mission hall for St David's Church in Beaufort and still used as such by the church.
Photo Keith Thomas.

Photos courtesy Kevin Sutton

Norwegian Church, Swansea, Wales

Originally sited in Newport, Gwent, the Grade 2 listed Norwegian Church was moved to Swansea Docks in circa 1910. Located between adjacent railways to the north and east, buildings to the south, and a road to the west, it initially comprised a Church and Mission, with a Vestry soon added to the north, the route of the existing railway explaining the peculiar 'splay' to this corner. A further extension to the south of the church was added relatively recently. It is one of the last surviving examples in Wales of a seamen's mission church and illustrates the close historical links that once existed between the South Wales seaports and Norway, and which resulted in the growth of a significant Norwegian community within this part of the world. The Church is currently empty, in a dilapidated state with the exterior having been cement rendered and it now requires considerable repair and restoration before being able to be put to any practical use. Fortunately however this work is being undertaken as part of a scheme to economically regenerate the docks area of Swansea. The building will be dismantled, relocated and restored and used as an attractive 'gateway' visitor centre to the newly redeveloped Port Tawe.

Ysgoldy Bach (The Little School House), Cwm Ceirig, Mathafarn, near Machynlleth is in excellent condition and has recently been refurbished. There are very few of these tiny school buildings left but they must have been quite common in rural areas at the end of the nineteenth century.

St Thomas Church, Pantbach Road, Cardiff

This is a tin church which has been recently refurbished including exterior cladding in modern roof material (possibly PVC). Features small steeple, arched windows at rear, arched double door at front.

The origins of St Thomas Church go back to about 1911 when a small body of Anglicans met for worship above a shop in Birchgrove, Cardiff. Birchgrove is within walking distance of both St Mary's and Gabalfa Church, and this group was probably a church mission for the newly formed suburb of Birchgrove. The Diocese had appointed a Diocesan Missioner following Archbishop Benson's Mission in Wales (1886-89), "...for reviving the clergy and renewing the laity." In June 1913, the men of the Birchgrove mission group cleared the land, craftsmen built the foundations, and the present 'iron' church was quickly erected. This had been moved from Whitchurch Hospital, as the hospital had built a handsome church to replace it. On 24th November, 1913 the first service was held at the church. This mission church was designed to seat 200 at a tight squeeze. In 1927, the chancel was added together with the vestries. The Church Hall was built some time later. The carefully tended grounds were also used as a tennis court.

Abandoned mission hall on the side of the A485 near Tregaron in West Wales.

This building has not been used for a very long time but the old harmonium and some of the pews were still inside when it was spotted and photographed.

Hall at Hundleton, Pembrokeshire

This hall now used for church meetings probably originated as an army accommodation quarters although Hundleton originally had a spectacular iron church which was demolished in the 1930s (see page 12).

Unity Labour Hall, Fishguard, Wales

Beautiful little hall of the type built across the country as mission halls.
Almost certainly religious use originally as the windows have been changed
from gothic arch openings as seen in the photo to rectangular windows.
Was opened as the Fishguard Unity Labour Hall in 1955
by Clement Atlee. Before that is served as a school
building for some time. In excellent condition, front
recently painted although the back had not
received quite the same amount of care.

Main Street Chapel, Frodsham, Cheshire

The busy evangelical church in the middle of the thriving Cheshire town of Frodsham. Quite extensive modern additions to the front and rear of the church have not disguised its more humble origins. The roofed bell tower looks like an original fitting as it is carefully blended into the roofline.

Eastbrook Methodist Church, Chapel Row, Dinas Powys, South Glamorgan

This interesting little tin chapel was originally built as a mission church for the
navvies working on the Barry Railway. It was taken over by the Wesleyans in
1887 and is still in regular daily use today not only as a church and Sunday
School but also as a daily playgroup centre and as the headquarters of the local
Brownies troop.

Tin Church, Eglwysfach, Ceredigion, Wales

Just a few miles south of Machynlleth on the A487 this picturesque corrugated iron church can be found at the side of the road (Eglwysfach translates from the Welsh into 'small church').

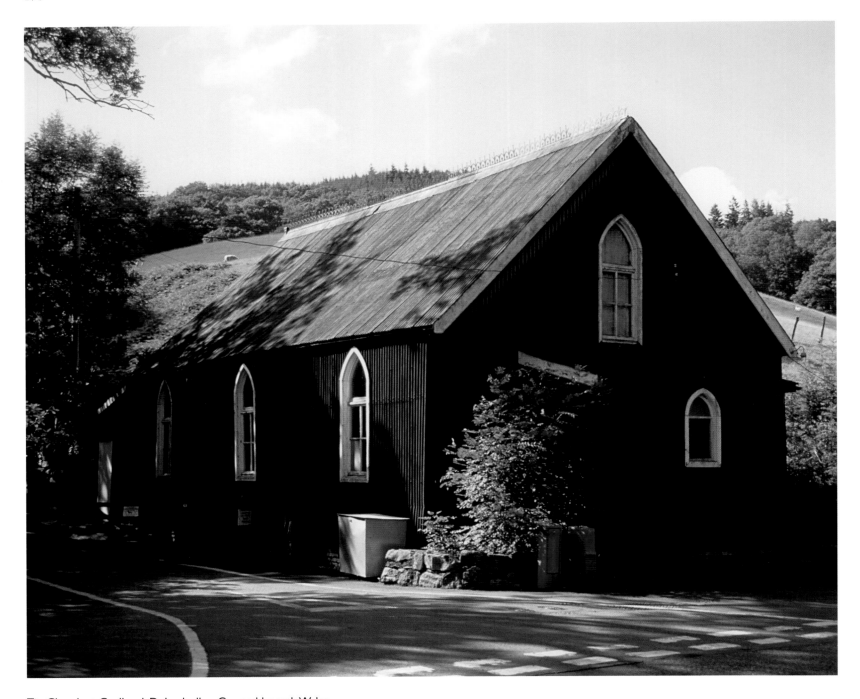

Tin Church at Ganllwyd, Dolmelynllyn, Gwynedd, north Wales

Nicely situated large tin church painted black with neat white trim next to a
woodland walk managed by the National Trust about 4 miles north of Dolgellau
on the A470 road. This building is obviously in regular use – the paintwork is in
excellent condition, the cast iron ridge decorations are intact and a glimpse
through the window showed a well kept interior.

The Church of the Good Shepherd, Drury, Flintshire, north Wales

This photogenic little corrugated iron church in north Wales is set in a beautiful well tended garden. The church features an interesting multi-angled two storey rear as the grounds slope steeply at the back.

Tin Church, White Grit, Shropshire/Powys border

This imposing corrugated iron church has recently been repainted so it should
be good for another few decades.
Photos Alan Terrill

All Saints Church, Pant y Gog, Garw Valley, South Wales

Captured on a misty morning in very early light, this is one of what were reputed to be hundreds of tin mission churches set up in the mining valleys of South Wales during the era of the great religious revivals. It must have been far easier to erect buildings like these on the slopes of the valleys than it would have been to erect 'proper' churches.

Ex mission hall at Clynderwen, Wales

This colourful corrugated building in the middle of the West Wales village of
Clynderwen has been converted for use as a home while retaining most of its
original features. Note the little clover leaf skylight above the front porch.

Meadows Road Gospel Hall, Crosshands, Carmarthenshire, Wales

This delightful little gospel mission hall discovered just behind a retail centre on the A48 to west Wales was demolished towards the end of 2003. It will be replaced with new housing.

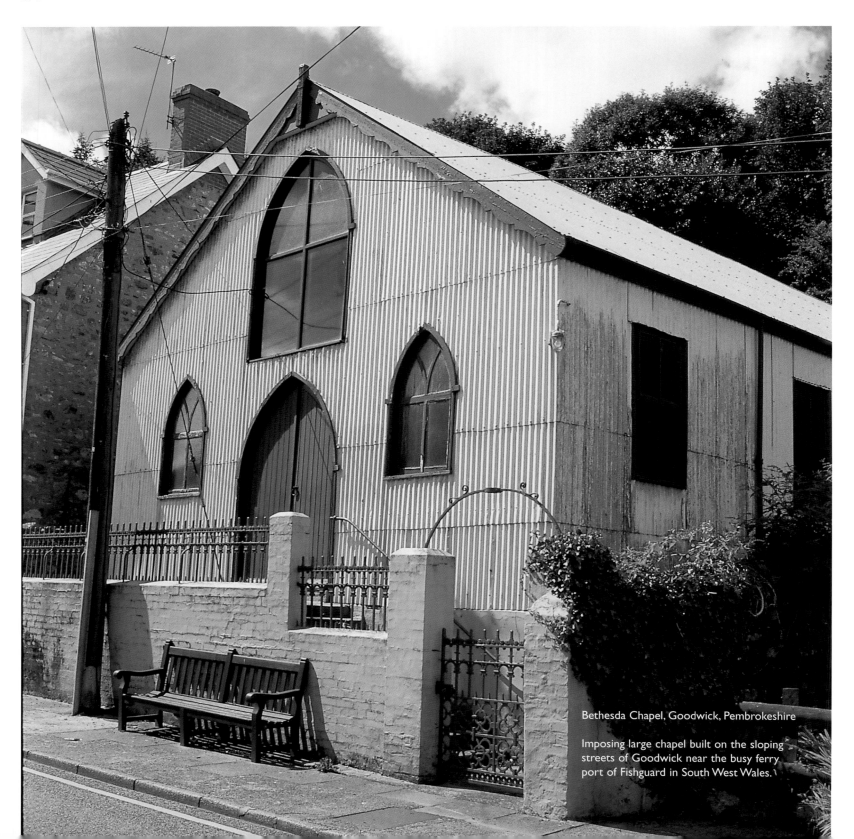

Bethesda Chapel, Goodwick, Pembrokeshire

Imposing large chapel built on the sloping
streets of Goodwick near the busy ferry
port of Fishguard in South West Wales.

St John's Church, Oakwood, Pontrhydyfen, South Wales

This large church built in 1883 has provided its community with sterling service for many years but it looks like the end is nigh for the building in this recent photograph. The old postcard on the left shows what it used to look like.

Tin Church, Pensarn, near Abergele, north Wales

The beautiful tin church of Church in Wales St Asaph diocese, fully restored using (perhaps unfortunately) modern box section corrugated iron. It still looks well proportioned with a small steeple at one end.

Glanrhyd Mission, Ystradgynlais, Swansea Valley

The little mission building in Glanrhyd, seen here on a bleak and wet autumn day,
is now used by the local Women's Institute. The windows have been replaced,
perhaps unsympathetically, with uPVC double glazing. It was originally called in
Welsh 'Eglwys Duw' which simply means 'God's Church'.

Capel Arenig, Arenig, Bala, north Wales

The corrugated iron chapel at Arenig near Bala in north Wales was recently sold as a property worth considering for use as a 'Walking Hostel, Boat Storage, etc'. The previous owner had installed an interesting home made heating system but prior to about 1986 the chapel was owned by the Calvinistic Methodist Church of Wales. In keeping with its former use, covenants are filed with the Land Registry to prevent the property from being used as a 'licensed premises, club, saloon or hall in which intoxicating liquor may be sold or consumed or for the purpose of betting, gaming or wagering'.

Beulah Mission Hall, north of Bridgend, South Wales

This busy mission hall in the Welsh valleys offers two prayer meetings and a Sunday School every Sunday as well as a Thursday service.

Church hall seen in the Rhondda Valley, South Wales

This hall at Cefn Cribwr has been clad in modern box section steel sheets and is used regularly as the local community centre.

Capel Sinc (Zinc Chapel) on the A487 north of Corris has definitely seen better days. Even though it is well hidden behind trees on the steeply sloped side of a busy road it has still been heavily vandalised. All of the windows have been broken and attempts at boarding the building up have not been a deterrent. The roof is not original but some of the fittings, like the cast iron ridge decorations, have been retained. The interior is in remarkable condition; on a building like this one would expect to see more evidence of deterioration and considering the amount of exterior vandalisation, it is a minor miracle that the piano and other fittings are still intact. As befits the area in which the chapel is situated, it sits on a sturdy foundation of Welsh slate.

St Matthias' Church, Glen Road, Belfast

This large church was recently under threat of demolition. Opened in 1892 as
the Church of Ireland's St Luke's Mission and subsequently re-consecrated as a
Catholic Church in 1970, this is one of only a few tin church buildings still
standing in northern and southern Ireland. Other examples in the north include
the small 1923 Gospel Hall in Glenanne and apparently a few others which have
been listed in the Silent Valley and Fermanagh. In the south there is the
marvellous 'Swiss Church' at Laragh, St Patrick's in Greenore and one at Sallins,
Co Kildare.

Photo Simon Knott

Chapter 6

Church of Ireland 'Swiss Church', Laragh, Co Monaghan, Republic of Ireland

The corrugated iron church at Laragh is noteworthy as a particluarly fine example of architecture in its own right. It sits in beautiful purpose designed landscaped grounds set in a narrow wooded valley with its own river. The three stage ornate spire with its little weather vane is an incongruous delight when compared to the usual heavy stone aesthetics of Irish church architecture. The church was apparently erected on the whim of the local mill owner and his wife who saw something similar in Switzerland during their honeymoon in the late 1800s (a typically Irish tale states that it was actually brought back from Switzerland but it is almost certainly a standard design industrial iron church with a few decorative additions). It is certainly reminiscent of Swiss wooden mountain chalets and it adds a very picturesque and magical element to the landscape of Laragh.

Photo courtesy of www.archeire.com (Irish Architecture Online)

IRELAND

There are now very few iron churches left standing in Ireland. The two pictured here, one from the north and one from the Republic show that some were built – in fact the famous Belfast engineering and ship building company Harland & Wolf is known to have dabbled in corrugated iron buildings – but few have survived.

In the north like many other parts of the UK corrugated iron has become part of the architectural vernacular and iron structures can be seen everywhere but few are churches.

In Eire the story is slightly different as the Republic has always retained its rural charm and even though corrugated iron has also played its part here in the form of agricultural buildings, barns, sheds and warehousing, the building of iron churches never reached the numbers seen outside Eire. However a number of iron churches were erected including, in the Dublin area the Church of Our Lady of Mercy, Artane, the Church of Our Lady of Consolation, Donnycarney and the Church of the Holy Child, Larkhill – none of these survive. Perhaps because the Republic never experienced the revivals and non-conformism in the same way as the other parts of the UK the need for these new buildings never occurred to the same extent even when the Republic was ostensibly under the rule of the British Crown.

Seventh Day Adventist Church, Blacking Street, Beaconsfield, South Africa

This church founded by an Afrikaans farmer in 1885 is regarded as the mother
of all Seventh Day Adventist Churches across South Africa and Australia/New
Zealand.

Chapter 7
OVERSEAS

As noted earlier, these corrugated iron prefabricated buildings were exported around the world but especially to the colonies of the British Empire. Many of the former colony countries have examples of these buildings. Several can be viewed in Australia and New Zealand and a very large iron church stood in San Francisco at the end of the nineteenth century. There are even some iron churches designed by Gustav Eiffel (Eiffel Tower, Paris) still to be found in Mexico and Gabon in Africa. These are cast iron rather than corrugated but some of the best preserved can be found in South Africa.

Seventh Day Adventist Church

A farmer by the name of Pieter Wessels founded the first Seventh Day Adventist church. He owned the farm Benaauwheidsfontein, the present site of the Wesselton Diamond Mine, and was a devout member of the Dutch Reformed Church. As time went by his

religious beliefs conflicted with those of his church and he decided to form his own denomination.

In 1885 Wessels sold the farm and established his own denomination with the proceeds. A small corrugated iron church was built on the corner of Blacking Street and Dyer Place in the municipality of Beaconsfield. This church is regarded as the mother church of all Seventh day Adventists in South Africa and Australia and it was from here that the new religious community grew and spread.

Lutheran Church of Saint Martin

In 1845 a Lutheran Mission was established at Pniel and it

is here that the Reverend Carl Meyer served before he became Kimberley's first Lutheran pastor. In the beginning the services were held in the High Court of Griqualand West but as the congregation grew in size the need for their own building became essential.

In 1875 the church was erected in Thompson Street. The building materials were especially imported via Port Elizabeth and transported to Kimberley by ox-drawn wagon. Saint Martin's remained the main church for the Lutheran community in Kimberley until 3 March 1963 when it was replaced by a new building in Lawson Street.

Even though the church is no longer used on a regular basis it can be seen with all its original fittings at the Open Mine Museum. Services are held there by special arrangement including weddings. Even now the church still has a role to play in Kimberley's history.

The Church at Skard, Iceland

Chapter 8
AN ICELANDIC ASIDE

Some of the tin churches in the UK were built as seamen's missions near ports. There is still one near Swansea Harbour and one in what is now the Cardiff Bay area. Both were clad in tin and both had Scandinavian connections. While looking into the history of these churches I came across some information about Iceland and it appeared that many of the churches built there were metal clad. I have since been informed that nearly all of the metal clad churches were originally built entirely from timber during the mid to late nineteenth century but the maintenance problems associated with timber cladding combined with the fact that Iceland had been practically stripped bare of timber (a massive re-forestation programme has been underway for many years) led to the timber being replaced with metal sheets. A few of the churches remain with the traditional corrugated galvanised sheets as used on most UK tin tabernacles, but most have since been updated using more modern material of the kind used for industrial buildings. This sheeting has more of a box section with less curves and probably better withstands the heavy snowfalls and build up of ice during the long winter months. Recent tendencies in preservation in Iceland have led some of the parishes to have their corrugated sheeting removed to be replaced with the original lapped timber cladding.

The amazing thing about these picture book churches is not just how many of them exist in a country which is relatively small but the fact that they are all kept in such pristine condition. As you can see from the pictures which illustrate just a very few of the Icelandic churches, each

15. Strandarkirkja.

This postcard from 1928 shows the church of Strandarkirkja, Iceland clad in corrugated iron. Note the peculiar shape of the chimney pipe running across the roof.

one is a little masterpiece. The detailing is usually much more elegant than that found on the UK tin tabernacles. Note the workmanship of the crosses on top of the towers and the attention to detail found in the surrounding fences or walls. The doors and windows are well made – perhaps they need to be to keep out the bitter winter cold. The windows are often small probably for the same reason. Many of these churches have an interesting spire or bell tower and the shapes of these vary from quite normal to extremely spindly or curvy extravaganzas which would look just as at home atop an ornate eastern orthodox church building. Perhaps it is simply that the landscapes in Iceland are themselves alien and exotic but these little churches, often standing alone in the middle of a field or on the edge of town have a poignancy which echoes the feeling one has coming across yet another abandoned and rusting UK tin church. The difference is that the Icelanders are making strenuous efforts to preserve their unique architectural heritage because they understand its value to the tourism industry. They also know that the preservation of buildings like these engenders some kind of patriotic appeal which the Icelanders themselves can feel part of.

Brautarholtskirkja, Iceland

This church would have been built and clad entirely in timber. As the timber rotted away it was replaced with corrugated iron to make maintenance easier but it has recently been renovated and the original timber cladding has been restored.

The Church at
Koströnd,
Iceland

Bibliography

Peter Ackroyd, *London: The Biography*, Vintage, 2001

Doreen M. Acton, *A History of Brentwood Baptist Church*, Brentwood Baptist Church, 1986

David Russell Barnes, *People of Seion*, Gwasg Gomer, 1995

JH Bettey, *Church and Parish: A Guide for Local Historians,* Batsford, 1987

Paul Dadson, *Context 44*, The Institute of Historic Building Conservation

John Dixon, *Look Back in Wonder*, Woodside Baptist Church, 1998

Gilbert Herbert, *Pioneers of Prefabrication*, The John Hopkins University Press, 1978

Pamela Horn, *The Victorian Country Child*, Alan Sutton Publishing, 1990

Liz Induni, *Tin Tabernacles*, article in Historic Churches Ninth Annual Edition, Cathedral
Communications Ltd, 2002

Pauline Johns, *Caterham Baptist Church: The First Hundred Years*, Caterham Baptist Church, 1994

Anthony Jones, *Welsh Chapels*, Alan Sutton Publishing in association with National Museums &
Galleries of Wales, 1996

Brynmor Pierce Jones, *How Lovely Are Thy Dwellings*, Wellspring, 1999

Joanna Power, *St Paul's, Warren Row: a History of the Church & Village*, Published by the Church,
1994

Donald Thomas, *The Victorian Underworld*, John Murray, 1998

David Thomson, *Europe Since Napoleon,* Pelican, 1957

Peter Wardle, *100 Years at Clows Top: A short history of the Mission Room*, 1995

Anne Warr, *Material Evidence Conserving Historic Building Fabric, Roofing: Corrugated Iron -
Options for Repair or Replacement*, Seminar Report, NSW Heritage Office, April 2000

N. Williams, *Quarry Bank*, Sutton Publishing, 1998

Tal Williams, *Salem Y Llun a'r Llan*, Cyhoeddiadus Barddas, 1991

Anthony Wood, *Nineteenth Century Britain 1815-1914*, Longman, 1982

Churches to Visit in Scotland, Saint Andrew Press, 2000

Durham Archaelogical Journal, Vol 6, 1990

Heritage Review, No 4, Ulster Architectural Heritage Society, Spring 2001

The Independent, 02.09.1992

The Independent, 24.05.1995

Monks to Millennium: The Story of the Village of Cilffriw, Cillfriw Millennium Book Group, 2000

The Oxford Dictionary of World Religions, ed. John Bowker, Oxford University Press, 1997

Sunday at Home 1907-8, The Religious Tract Society

The Telegraph, 18.08.2001

Western Mail, 01.02.2001

Worcestershire Recorder, No 63, Spring 2001

Index